MW00779701

Millionaire Mindset and Success Habits

How to Overcome Your Own Limiting Beliefs That Make You Stand in Your Own Way to Becoming Financially Free

H.J. Chammas

AUTHORITY
PUBLISHING

ISBN (Paperback): 979-8-5906-2273-3

ISBN (Hardcover): 979-8-9897577-7-0

Published by: Authority Publishing

www.authority-publishing.com

Printed in the United States of America.

Disclaimer

This book is designed to provide educative information and motivation to readers. The author and publisher are not offering it as legal, accounting, or other professional services advice. The methods described in this book are the sole expression and opinion of the author. They are not intended to be a definitive set of instructions. You may discover other methods and materials that accomplish the same end result. No warranties or guarantees are expressed or implied by the publisher's choice to include any of the content in this volume. Neither the publisher nor the author shall be liable for any physical, psychological, emotional, financial, or commercial damages, including, but not limited to, special, incidental, consequential, or other damages.

Our views and rights are the same: You are responsible for your own choices, actions, and results. Seek the services of a competent professional before beginning any self-improvement program.

Characters' names and identifying details have been changed to protect the privacy of individuals. Any likeness to actual persons, either living or dead, is strictly coincidental.

References are provided for informational purposes only and do not constitute an endorsement of any websites or other sources. The websites listed in this book may change.

Message from the Author

Two great mentors who have helped me transform my life taught me on different and unrelated occasions that "I am being my self-enemy." I did not understand what they both meant back then, although both occasions were almost four years apart.

Could it have taken me more than four years to understand this simple message? My inner beliefs are making me stand in my own way to success. In fact, it took me 35 years of my whole life and about 17 years of my adult life to understand this simple truth: our brain is designed to protect us and, therefore, makes us believe that we have limited capabilities to break out of our comfort zone and achieve success by simply doing things differently.

When I was in my mid-thirties, I was still financially poor, running from one paycheck to the other and practically working very hard for money—well, I worked very hard for the money that rarely remained in my pocket or bank account by the end of each month. I was a wage slave, and this by itself made me strongly adhere to many limiting beliefs that were making me stand in my own way to success.

When the financial crisis of 2008 and the COVID-19 pandemic of 2020 hit the whole world like two giant tsunami waves, I witnessed very close friends and colleagues being kicked out of their jobs and then could no longer sustain their standards of living. They were forced to downgrade their living standards until they found another job. Finding another job often took weeks and months for most to accept and settle for a lower salary. So, practically, even after finding another job, they were forced to downgrade their lifestyle indefinitely until one day they would have more money than they had always wished.

Witnessing how many had struggled when they were laid off by their employers in 2008 made me wake up to the realization that if I don't break out from the money habit of working hard for money, one day, I might face the same destiny as those who had only the option to downgrade their standard of living. Without a blink of an eye, I started researching the success habits of the rich and wealthy. My thorough research made me understand their mindset and how they are programmed. I started adopting all those habits, and my mindset was being transformed daily until I changed my financial reality and became financially independent in a short span of seven years.

The 2020 pandemic was also a big hit on the whole world. It weakened the world economy, leaving employers no choice but to downsize and restructure their operations to fit their lower turnover. In retrospect, I feel blessed that I was not depending on a job to earn a living. I feel blessed to be able to help thousands of others improve their financial well-being through the help of my courses and books found on www .employeemillionaire.com.

When I started my journey to financial independence, I was in my mid-30s, and I felt I might have missed the chance to improve my finances; however, my determination to become wealthy pushed me to overcome my own limiting beliefs. I studied many books and sought the help of coaches and mentors who have already achieved what I want to achieve in my life. I overcame my obstacles and created a new reality in my life-attaining financial freedom, becoming a millionaire, and living the life I always dreamt of.

The route I have selected to improve my finances from a financial disaster to one of financial freedom was investing in income-producing assets, specifically real estate. Rental property has an advantage over other investment vehicles in the following areas:

- The use of leverage.

- Cash Flow.

- Control.

- Liquidation of profits without the need to sell the property.

All those advantages, as well as other important ones, are beyond the scope of this book. They were covered in full in my award-winning best-selling book - *The Employee Millionaire Real Estate Investor: How to Build Wealth, Grow Rich, and Become an Everyday Millionaire with Rental Property Investing*. This unique book will help you produce positive financial results in your life without the need for you to leave your job. Isn't this amazing?

Although my investment preference is rental properties, the lessons shared in this book apply to any route you might select for your wealth-building process.

The main reason I wrote this book is '*purpose*.' My experience in life, business, and relations has helped me identify my purpose in life, which is adding value to people's lives. I was fortunate enough to learn from many others, so I wanted to pass this knowledge on, hoping it will help you achieve financial freedom and a better quality of life.

Download the Free Resources That Come With This Book

Go to the link below, and you'll be able to gain access to a whole vault of valuable resources that I refer to in this book, including:

1. *Personal Financial Statement*: This comes with a Financial KPIs Dashboard to help you understand your finances and track your financial progress.

2. *Loan Eligibility Calculator*: to determine your creditworthiness to finance the purchase of assets.

3. *Loan Payment Calculator*: to keep track of your payments, remaining balance, and the whole payment schedule.

4. *Your Big Why List*: a template designed to help you spell out the real reasons you want to change your life and finances.

5. *The Rental Properties Investment Blueprint*: summarizes the steps you must undertake to prospect, finance, own, rent, and manage rental properties for positive cash flow.

www.employeemillionaire.com/breakout-resources

Those resources are designed to allow you to implement all the strategies in this book to your personal situation.

Free Copy of My Bestselling Book on Personal Finance

This book *includes a complimentary copy of my bestselling personal finance book, The 4 Stages Of Building Wealth.*

I intentionally wanted to keep this book short and crisp; therefore, I avoided including additional essential lessons on the "how-to" of personal finance.

You can download your copy instantly from www.employeemillionaire.com/the4stages.

Download the Audio Version of This Book Free

If you love listening to audiobooks on the go or would enjoy narration as you read along, I have great news for you.

You can switch back and forth between reading and listening so that you don't stop whenever it's not convenient to read.

You can download the audiobook version of *Millionaire Mindset and Success Habits* by signing up for a free 30-day Audible trial!

Click the links below to get started:

For Audible US: https://www.audible.com/pd/B08WW27Y89

For Audible UK: https://www.audible.co.uk/pd/B08WVRWC9X

Contents

Chapter One
What is Your "Big Why"?

Before thinking about setting your goals, building your plan, and working on executing your plan, if you haven't yet thought about the things you want in life, you're missing a main pillar of success. This is often referred to as your "Big Why" list.

The longer you think, the clearer your vision becomes. The further you look into the future, five or ten years, the less prejudgment you will have on whether your ambitions are achievable. You will discover that your list may include both personal and financial ambitions.

Once, my mentor asked me to imagine a reporter interviewing me ten years in the future and then reflecting on what I would like them to write about me—my personal and career achievements. I encourage you to do the same exercise. I promise it's going to be fun!

Open up a blank document on your device and start imagining what this reporter will write about your life ten years later. Don't judge what you will be writing about. Just write down the things you envision yourself achieving in this time horizon.

If you examine the common threads on your list, you may realize that they are all somehow interrelated and can be regrouped into the following areas of life:

- Home and family

- Health and fitness

- Work, career, and finances

- Personal development and education

- Social life and relationships

- Spiritual development and life contribution

When I did this exercise, it was a remarkable discovery that my personal life ambitions came first, before my financial ambitions. I discovered that my financial ambitions acted as enablers for me to achieve my personal life ambitions.

My "Big Why" List	

Name: _____ Date: / /

Things I want in life	Areas of Life *

* Areas of Life Guidelines:
- Home & Family
- Health & Fitness
- Work, Career & Finances
- Personal Development & Education
- Social Life & Relationships
- Spiritual Development and Life Contribution
- Others: Please create names for the areas of life not listed above

Figure 1 - My "Big Why" List

To help you create your "Big Why" list, you can use a template, which you can download for free from my website. Here is the link: www.employee millionaire.com/breakout-resources.

You can start by writing whatever comes to your mind without any particular order. Then, you can categorize the things you want in your life into their respective areas of life. Your time spent here is very well spent to have a crystal clear vision of what you want in your life.

Suppose you want to take this exercise to the next level, especially if you are a person who prefers to visualize things in photos (and videos). In that case, you can translate your "Big Why" list to a vision board using any graphics tool you prefer.

Chapter Two
Are We All Programmed?

WHEN I WAS A teenager, I always wondered why my parents were so adamant about their children seeking higher education so that they would get secure, high-paying jobs. My parents have spent their adult lives as employees, going through the ups and downs of the employee life. They were, at times, put out of their jobs and then forced to pay for less-paying and less rewarding jobs. They worked very hard for money to provide the best they could for their family. When they retired, they realized that neither their previous employer nor the government would look after them. My parent retired broke, and luckily enough, I had the means to take care of their needs when they were out of money after their legal retirement age.

During my childhood, I observed that the parents of my wealthy classmates did things quite differently from the route my parents selected for themselves. When I used to visit their houses for play days, even as a young child, it was obvious to me that my wealthy classmates' lifestyle was quite far from the lifestyle our family was enjoying—or not enjoying!

When I grew a bit more mature, I automatically fell into the same "life programming," As soon as I graduated, I started my career in the corporate world. I was trapped in the rat race, running from one paycheck to the next. My corporate life allowed me great exposure to working with my colleagues worldwide. I also have worked as an expatriate in different countries for almost 17 years. I realized that almost all my work colleagues, irrespective of where they fall on the corporate ladder and which country they live and work in, had accepted their fate and were trying to make the most out of the life program their parents handed them.

When I started my wealth-building journey, my starting point was taking a proper inventory of my financial situation. When I looked at my first-ever personal financial statement, dozens of questions and ideas came to my mind. Sometimes, I comforted myself with some irrational justifications for my financial ruin. It was like covering a bad story with another bad story. Finally, I had to face reality and objectively analyze what brought me to this situation. During this same time, I looked at Forbes's list of billionaires and asked myself how those billionaires and other wealthy people attract money like a magnet. In contrast, people like me, my fellow colleagues, and employees in general seem to repel it.

Determined to discover the answers, I talked to dozens of people, including ones who were poor, middle-class, well-off, and wealthy. As I met people who were low-, medium-, and high-paid employees, self-employed, investors, and business owners, I began to notice that people who depend on earned income, irrespective of their income level, have much in common. On the other hand, people who have acquired multiple income streams from their income-producing assets also share a lot in common. The difference between those classes was astonishing.

People who have accumulated wealth have let go of many misconceptions and limiting beliefs. The wealthy have managed to subscribe to a new set of empowering beliefs contradicting what the majority of the population still hangs onto.

It appears that we are all programmed to believe in a set of false assumptions that become limiting beliefs. Too often, the poor and the middle class hold tightly to limiting beliefs about money and investing. Meanwhile, those same beliefs hold them captive and prevent them from achieving financial freedom.

When I first looked at my personal financial statement, I had the same limiting beliefs. It was only when I understood how those beliefs were enslaving me to a state of financial ruin that I managed to let go of them. I had to understand the personal truth about my negative thoughts to overcome them and replace them with empowering beliefs.

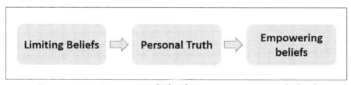

Figure 2—Limiting beliefs vs. empowering beliefs

Let's go through those beliefs and see how the poor and middle class look at them differently—actually in opposite ways. The poor and the middle class have adopted limiting personal beliefs, whereas the wealthy have adopted empowering personal beliefs. You'll never embark on the road to wealth if you let such negative thoughts constrain you.

The poor and the middle class will most probably remain in the same financial situation if they conjure up any number of excuses for not choosing wealth—excuses that say more about their inner thoughts than about the difficulty of achieving wealth.

If you're embracing negative thoughts, you need to understand what they really mean. It's time to dig deep and unearth your personal truths. Jot down negative statements you whisper to yourself, and, after some honest soul searching, record the personal truth beneath each. Once you become honest with yourself and accept that those beliefs are limited only to the extent you allow them to be, you will experience a transformation of those beliefs into empowering ones. Self-awareness is critical in this transformation. Before you change your life, you need to change your mind. Your thoughts and beliefs are so deeply entrenched that you may not even be aware of how much they've impacted your financial situation.

Chapter Three

Limiting Belief: A Job Provides Financial Security for Now and at Retirement

BEFORE BECOMING WEALTHY, I started as a poor man and improved my situation to an average middle-class person. This was my life for most of my life until I reached my early 40s. I have colleagues and friends who are poor and middle-class, and without exceptions, we've all been programmed to graduate from school to seek a high-paying job that would provide us security and eventually lead to wealth. Here is the thing: This might hold for the top of the corporate pyramid, with CEOs and other corporate executives with hefty paychecks. Those C-level executives are the smallest population of any corporation. To most employees, this remains a dream they chase until one day they retire, only to be surprised by a bank account and pension plan that can barely sustain their lifestyle for a few weeks or months. Then reality kicks in—when it is too late. The fact is that a job, for most of us, merely supports the basics of life, the essential expenses.

The drug that keeps all employees addicted to their jobs is seeing their income increase from the day they start working till the prime of their income-earning years. This false evidence of prosperity leads to a false feeling of security. As a result, more and more of their income gets channeled to discretionary expenses, and those who can afford it start to spend on the appearance of wealth. One day, their income starts to go downhill, and like a drug addict who cannot have the same high doses of drugs anymore, they wake up to the fact that this fantasy is over and that they must cut down on their expenses.

The graph below shows the general population's earned income trend over time. If you want to learn more about this topic, I recommend reading books by Harry S. Dent Jr., an economist specializing in generational consumer income and spending patterns.

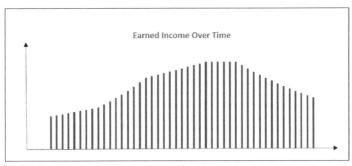

Figure 3—Earned income over time

I encourage you to start looking at your job differently. Instead of seeing it as working harder and harder for your employer's benefit, consider it a form of leverage that acts in your favor. It is about having your job work smarter for you while you work hard for your job. It's a win-win arrangement.

In one of my coaching programs, *The Four Pillars of Wealth*, I have shared a detailed plan that allows students to leverage their employment to qualify for bank loans (good debt) to purchase income-producing assets that will generate unearned income over their monthly expenses and, therefore, put them on the road to building wealth. You can check out this life-changing program at www.employeemillionaire.com/fourpillarscourse.

This is a win-win arrangement with lenders and financial institutions. You make money on your investments (in the form of both unearned income and capital gains), while they make money by charging you interest on the money they lend you. Banks like to lend money to creditworthy people. They want reasonable reassurance that borrowers have steady incomes that will enable them to repay their loans. Banks will look at how long the borrowers were in their current jobs as their reassurance of steady income.

The dynamics of qualifying for bank loans to finance your investments are beyond the scope of this book. Given the importance of this topic, I would like to gift you a free electronic copy of my best-selling book—*The Four Stages of Building Wealth*. You can download your copy now from this link:

www.employeemillionaire.com/the4stages.

The first step of the wealth-building process is to take advantage of the fact that you have a steady income that qualifies you for a loan that you can take to purchase income-producing assets.

I invite you now to reprogram your own limiting belief about your job providing you financial security. Below is a guide on reprogramming your thought process. You will need to give it a deep thought and rewrite it with your own words that reflect your current set of beliefs.

Limiting Belief: A job provides financial security for now and at retirement.

Personal Truth: I don't want to give up the feeling of security of earning a regular paycheck. I can be kicked out of my job at any time.

Empowering Belief: I need to be in control of my future income. I can leverage my position as an employee to qualify for *good debt* to purchase income-producing assets that will generate *unearned income*.

Chapter Four

Limiting Belief: Debt is Bad

CARRYING A CREDIT CARD back in the eighties was considered a privilege. Nowadays, credit card companies harass people with steady incomes by offering them free-for-life credit cards. Things have evolved so that you can take a cash advance with zero down payment and zero interest for several months. The trick here is that most people will fail to repay those credit card loans within the grace period and then get penalized with huge interest rates ranging from 24% to 36% per year. This is when the borrower becomes captive to those high-interest loans.

With good marketing campaigns that influence consumers' psychology, bankers and big companies are partnering to entice us to buy goods and services that will provide instant gratification. They are making it easy for consumers to get a suite of credit cards, personal loans, and car loans with reasonable monthly payments to make buying those goods and services a

no-brainer, even if we cannot afford them. It is normal to see offers
from retailers tempting consumers to use their credit cards to buy now
and pay later at zero interest over three, six, nine, or twelve months.
The caveat is that those goods and services are worthless when the debt
is repaid.

Most of us have fallen victim to tempting instant gratification offers
with delayed payment plans. We started to fear being captive to debt.
Our parents, the school, and the community have each taught us that
debt is bad and must be avoided at any cost. And they are correct when
it comes to *bad debt*. On the other hand, *good debt* incurred to purchase
income-producing assets sets you on the road to wealth.

In *The Four Stages of Building Wealth*, you will be introduced to a
non-conventional idea: "*You will become at least as rich as the amount
of good debt you take in your life.*" I would even dare to claim that
you can almost never become wealthy without incurring some form of
good debt. Think of it as borrowing yourself to wealth. Pay attention:
I mentioned *good debt*, which is the kind of debt you incur to purchase
income-producing assets.

The 4 Stages Of Building Wealth fully explains the difference between
good and bad debt. As a thank-you token for reading this book, I am
offering you a free eBook of The 4 Stages Of Building Wealth, which
can be downloaded from www.employeemillionaire.com/the4stages.

Now, going back to the point I was trying to drive a while ago, to
explain better the concept of the idea: "*You will become at least as rich
as the amount of good debt you take in your life.*" I am throwing at you
another one - "*The road to wealth is good debt.*"

You might think I am attempting to explain an obscure concept with another one!

Stay with me for a while.

Good debt, acquired to purchase income-producing assets, accelerates the road to wealth.

Here is a question: How many $100,000 properties can you purchase with $100,000 cash?

If your answer is only one property, you would fall into what most of the population would believe. Although this answer is mathematically correct, it is financially naïve.

Let's examine a couple of other options, which are both mathematically correct and financially wiser.

Before we do that, we need to set a common set of assumptions that can be applied to all the options I am about to share to obtain like-for-like comparisons easily.

1. Each property in any option is bought at the market price of $100,000.

2. The monthly rent is $1,000 (equivalent to $12,000 annually).

3. The monthly expenses are $100 (equivalent to $1,200 annually).

Option 1: The $100,000 home was purchased using all the investor's $100,000 in cash

In this scenario, the property's net cash flow, the *rental income* less the *total expenses*, is $10,800 ($12,000 – $1,200). This results in a 10.8% ROI on the investor's money, computed by dividing the net cash flow of $10,800 by the investor's invested capital of $100,000.

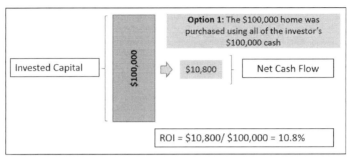

Figure 4—Property bought with 100% of investor's cash

Option 2: The $100,000 home was purchased using 20% of the investor's cash. A mortgage loan was taken to finance 80% of the property

In this scenario, the investor must pay a monthly mortgage to the bank towards the $80,000 loan taken. At an interest rate of 5% and loan terms of 30 years, the monthly mortgage payment will be $430, equivalent to $5,160 per year.

Mortgage payments can be calculated using many online mortgage calculators or by downloading the mortgage payments calculator in Microsoft Excel format from www.employeemillionaire.com/breakout-resources.

The resulting net cash flow will be $5,640 ($12,000 – $1,200 – $5,160), and the resulting ROI will be 28.2%. This is computed by dividing the $5,640 net cash flow by the investor's invested capital of $20,000.

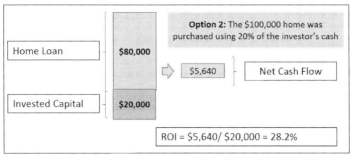

Figure 5—Property bought with 20% investor's cash and 80% mortgage loan

Option 3: The $100,000 home was purchased using none of the investor's cash. A mortgage loan was taken to finance 100% of the property

In this scenario, the investor must pay a monthly mortgage to the bank towards the $100,000 loan taken. At an interest rate of 5% and loan terms of thirty years, the monthly mortgage payment will be $537, equivalent to $6,444 per year. The resulting net cash flow will be $4,356 ($12,000 – $1,200 – $6,444). The resulting ROI will be infinite. This is computed by dividing $4,356 net cash flow over the investor's invested capital of $0.

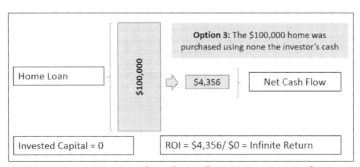

Figure 6—Property bought with 100% mortgage loan

This is where the magic happens. This is how infinite returns can be achieved. The investor will incur a zero-down payment in this deal. This was my first lesson on the power of leverage and the use of *good debt*. Indeed, the road to wealth is good debt.

Please note that I am not promoting zero-down payment deals, especially those bought at market price. My coaching program, *The Employee to Millionaire Real Estate Investor Course* (www.employeemillionaire.com/vcp), shares a process with practical steps to buy rental properties at a targeted 20% discounted price. That way, the price you will pay for rental property will equal 80% of its listed or market price. The difference between the price you will pay (80% of the market price) and the listed price of the property will be considered your 20% down payment when you take a loan for 80% of the property's value. Your knowledge and sweat equity for finding those good deals will equal the 20% down payment.

Warren Buffet explains how price does not equal value with his famous quote: "Price is what you pay, value is what you get." To better illustrate my point, let's revisit scenario three above, but this time, you have found a good deal at a 20% discount (the price of the property will be $80,000), and then upon applying for a loan, let's assume your banker will give you an 80% loan on the market value of the property. So, 80% of the market value of $100,000 will be $80,000. That way, the loan amount will be equivalent to the price you will pay for the property, namely $80,000. In that overly simplified example, the monthly net cash flow will be exactly as option two above, $5,640, but the ROI will be infinite since you have invested zero from your capital.

Now that I've demonstrated how leverage if applied correctly and wisely, could produce wealthy rates of returns, let me share one of the biggest secrets you're encouraged to grasp on your journey to financial independence.

"You will become at least as rich as the amount of good debt you take in your life."

When I first learned this concept, my brain started racing while figuring out what it could mean to my financial life. To bring this concept to life, if you want to receive $1 million in the future, you must borrow $1 million in *good debt*. Now, let us raise the numbers: if you want to receive $10 million in the future, you must borrow $10 million in good debt.

For the sake of simplicity, I am using a round figure of a $100,000 market value for a single-family house in the examples in this chapter. Real property values may be higher or lower depending on the country and the city you wish to invest in.

Imagine a $100,000 single-family house purchased with zero down payment. In this example, we would have incurred $100,000 in good debt, which was used to purchase the property.

If this house is rented out continuously throughout the loan and the loan is paid back, we will own 100% equity at the end of the loan terms, which is thirty years in our example. Even if we disregard all positive cash flow and price appreciation over the thirty years, we will own 100% equity in that house. This means we will own a home free and clear with a value of $100,000. This is exactly equivalent to the amount of the loan taken. This is only the start!

If we follow the purchase criteria of searching for properties discounted at 20%, the 80% loan-to-value will equal the property's price. This means that our equity in the property will be $20,000 on day one after we own the house.

With the same logic, keeping the house rented over the thirty-year duration of the loan will result in $100,000 equity, which is even higher than the loan amount. This also excludes any cash flow and capital appreciation over the thirty years. I trust you will deduce now how "you will become at least as rich as the amount of good debt you take in your life." Notice that I mentioned "at least."

The two examples above for the same property value show that the total equity gained was at least equal to the amount of the loan taken. The gains are much higher when we factor in the positive cash flow and capital gains in the long term.

I will dive deeper to answer any questions you might have about the examples I shared a while ago.

A mortgage is a long-term loan designed to help the borrower purchase a property. In addition to repaying the principal, the borrower must make interest payments to the lender, and the property around it serves as collateral. Every monthly mortgage payment is split between the principal and the interest. Loans are structured so that the principal amount returned to the borrower starts small and increases with each mortgage payment. A mortgage's interest rate directly impacts the mortgage payment's size, where higher interest rates mean higher mortgage payments. There is an inverse relationship between the loan term (the length of time within which the loan must be fully paid back) and the size of the monthly payment, with longer terms resulting in smaller monthly payments.

The graph below shows how the $537 monthly payment (equivalent to a $6,444 annual payment) is split between principal and interest over thirty years. This is the same monthly mortgage payment in option three in the example above.

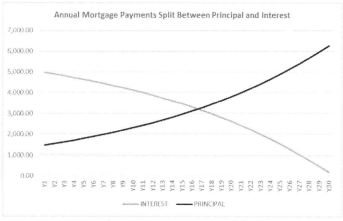

Figure 7—Annual mortgage payments split between principal and interest

Each principal payment adds to the borrower's equity, reducing the remaining loan balance. The graph below visually explains how equity accumulates over the loan's terms when monthly mortgage payments are paid back to the bank.

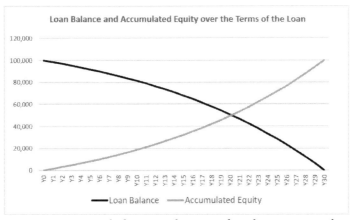

Figure 8—Loan balance and accumulated equity over the terms of the loan

The most interesting part of the story is that the investor doesn't need to wait the full thirty years, the term of the debt, to claim ownership of the full equity of $100,000. In just fifteen years, half of the term of the thirty-year loan, the investor could earn more than $100,000 in cash if the home appreciates at 5% per year. If we add a 5% appreciation for the price of the home per year, the home will more than double in value in fifteen years. To be exact, the home's value will be $207,893 in fifteen years.

In this example, appreciation is assumed to be a flat 5% yearly. Property prices move up, down, or sideways during a year, with a long-term appreciation averaging between 3 and 6% in most developed markets.

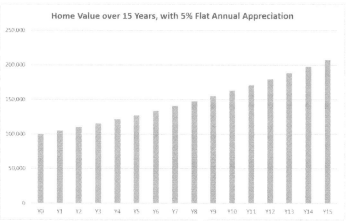

Figure 9—Home value over fifteen years, with a 5% flat annual appreciation

If the investor sells the home in fifteen years, the total money to be cashed out before tax will be $140,009, split as follows:

- The $107,893 profit—the difference between the appreciated price of $207,893 and the original price of $100,000.

- All the accumulated equity resulting from the loan payment over fifteen years. This will be equivalent to $32,116.

If the house is sold in exactly twelve years, the investor can earn a little over $100,000.

The graph below explains how the sum of the accumulated equity and the home appreciation can add up over the years to reap benefits for the investor. The assumption here is a flat 5% annual appreciation over fifteen years.

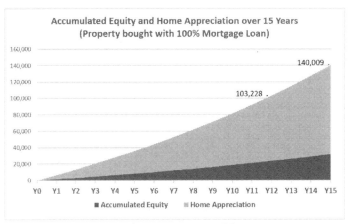

Figure 10—Accumulated equity and home appreciation
over fifteen years

The investor could also shorten the period to receive the full $100,000 in cash in less than twelve years. The investor could add all the $4,356 net cash flow from the property to the loan payment to accelerate the debt payment. Many banks allow a certain balloon payment per year, which could be capped to a certain percentage of the loan balance. This will speed up the payback of the loan by more than two-thirds. In that way, in exactly eight years, the home could be sold at $147,746 (with 5% annual appreciation), and the accumulated equity due to monthly loan payment and annual balloon payment will be $55,916. Adding both figures together will net the investor a handsome $103,662 in eight years. Not bad!

The graph below explains this scenario visually.

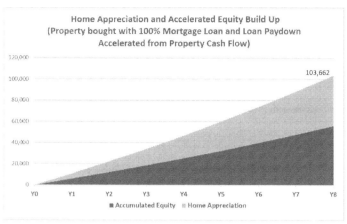

Figure 11—Home appreciation and accelerated equity build-up

To recap the above, debt is a form of leverage, specifically financial leverage. The power of leverage was greatly appreciated from the days BC, with the famous quote from Archimedes: *"Give me a lever long enough and a place to stand, and I will move the entire earth."*

Remember that to be wealthy, you need to use leverage, which means not only financial leverage, like money borrowed from a financial institution. Wise investors will also leverage non-financial resources like time, knowledge, and connections. Leveraging money and time are commonly referred to as OPM and OPT, which stand for "other people's money" and "other people's time," respectively. With this book, you are already leveraging my knowledge.

I invite you now to reprogram your own limiting belief about debt by following the guide below, but by rephrasing it with your own words.

Limiting Belief: Debt is bad. It signals captivity. I must avoid it at any cost.

Personal Truth: I have been captive to debt that I have taken towards the purchase of goods and services that will become worthless by the time the debt is paid.

Empowering Belief: I need to start investing in income-producing assets that will generate unearned income. I understand that debt allows for higher returns. I can never become wealthy without incurring some form of good debt in my life.

Chapter Five

Limiting Belief: Saving Your Money is the Wisest Investment

MOST RESPONSIBLE AND CARING parents advise their newly graduating adult children who are about to join the workforce and build their careers to ensure they save their hard-earned money in long-term savings plans that generate some interest. Our parents' advice is sound, but it can never lead to wealth if the saved money is never put to hard work by having it invested in income-producing assets that generate unearned income and build wealth.

Interest rates on saving accounts vary widely across countries, especially in local currencies. On average, interest earned on savings is below 3 percent for accounts. Let's see how many years it takes for $100,000 to double if deposited in a savings bank account at 3 percent interest.

In the 1400s, the Italians gave the world a method to estimate the doubling time of investment, often called the rule of 72. Rule number 72 is divided by the annual interest percentage to obtain the approximate number of years required for doubling. Although scientific formulas and calculations provide more accurate figures, the rule of 72 is quite useful for mental calculations or when only a basic calculator is available. Using the rule of 72 to compute how many years are required to double an amount of $100,000 deposited in a savings account at 3 percent annual interest, we divide 72 by 3. The result is twenty-four. So, it takes twenty-four years to double an amount stashed in a savings account at 3 percent interest.

$$T= 72/R= 72/3= 24$$

Let's now compute how many years it takes for money invested in an income-producing asset that generates 10 percent ROI to double. If we divide 72 over 10, we will get 7.2 years.

$$T= 72/R= 72/10= 7.2$$

If the ROI is 15 percent, the resulting number will be 4.8 years.

You will agree that it will take seemingly forever to double your money at low interest rates when saved in the bank. But it can take fewer years when the money is properly invested at double-digit returns. In the previous section of this book, we saw how investments can result in high double-digit ROI if properly invested in income-producing assets and with the use of leverage and good debt.

Is it possible that your money in the bank could be at 100% risk?

The short answer is "yes!"

I know you might be surprised and raise an eyebrow. You might think that the bank or the government protects money saved in the bank. This could be correct in certain countries, but up to a certain limit per account.

History tells us that many countries have defaulted in the past. If history predicts the future, other sovereign defaults are a possibility. This is a list of famous sovereign defaults: Lebanon (2020), Venezuela (2017), Greece (2015), Ecuador (2008), Argentina (2001), Russia (1998), Mexico (1994), France (1958), and Spain (more than 15 times by 1939).

The next question on your mind could be: what happens when a country defaults?

I will outline the potential consequences of a country defaulting and how it could impact your savings in the bank:

1. The country's currency can be devalued, which means the purchasing power of your savings will be reduced. This means your life savings will be worth much less.

2. Government debt can be restructured by extending the loan payment date, reducing the loan amount, or further devaluing the currency by printing more local currency.

3. Austerity measures might be followed, which include spending cuts and tax increases.

4. The living standards of people can also be impacted. It might start with street riots, leading to the banking crises. The core reason for banking crises can be that people might attempt to

take all their money out of the banks due to uncertainty and confusion. The government may close down the banks to avoid money withdrawals. Occasionally, withdrawal is permitted, but capital controls are imposed. Your money will be locked down in "money jail" (aka the bank), and it might take a few years to release.

5. Countries defaulting on foreign currency debt might also default on local currency debt. If you bought treasury bonds and the country defaults on foreign currency debt, you might not receive your bond periodic payments.

6. Turmoil can occur in the stock market due to uncertainty. No one might be willing to buy anything; many investors might even decide not to do business with the country until the situation is stable.

7. Governments may refuse to pay any money or reduce the borrowed money, as in Argentina in 2001.

8. The country can lose its reputation, and its rating might decline, making it harder to borrow money in the future.

9. GDP will contract, and a financial crisis is imminent. Banks will not lend money, and in the rare case they might do so, borrowing money will become too expensive.

This book is not intended to be a crash course on the economy, but I thought this information is crucial for you to grasp, especially if you believe saving money is the wisest investment.

Similar to how we approached the previous limiting beliefs, it's time for you now to rewrite your belief about saving your money in the bank. Below is how I rewired my brain about this topic.

Limiting Belief: Saving my money is the wisest investment.

Personal Truth: I am cynical about investment. I let fear rule my decisions. I need to educate myself on how to invest for higher returns.

Empowering Belief: Investments can result in high double-digit ROI if properly invested in income-producing assets and with the use of leverage.

Chapter Six

Limiting Belief: The Government and My Employer are Responsible for my Financial Well-being

THE BEST THING ABOUT history is that it helps us predict the future. In the last 100 years, there have been several recessions globally. The recent recessions we've witnessed were the global recession in 2008 and the pandemic in 2020. The well-documented facts show us that employees were laid off, and unemployment shot up to high double digits. Employers who had to let go of their employees never thought they were responsible for the financial well-being of those laid-off employees. To me, no job looks secure.

On the other hand, governments worldwide have genuine obligations to improve their economies and provide jobs for their citizens. They have attempted to boost their respective economies with quantitative easing and other forms of easy money so that companies will borrow money for free to invest in their businesses and recruit people. The result of lowering unemployment did take a long time. In most cases, although unemployment decreased in percentage, the quality of the jobs created and the respective paychecks were far from the levels before those recessions hit.

The fact of the matter is that you alone are responsible for your financial well-being. I encourage you to start changing your mindset and put yourself in control. I urge you to take advantage of your current employment status and invest in income-producing assets that will work hard for you to generate income. This unearned income will look after your well-being if you ever have to (or choose to) leave your current job.

You can choose the investment vehicle that best suits your personality and beliefs. I recommend investing in rental properties, and if you ever wish to learn more on the "how" of rental property investing, I invite you to check out my coaching course, *The Employee to Millionaire Real Estate Investor Course*, on www.employeemillionaire.com/vcp.

This course will guide you through the steps of investing in single-family rental properties, which will help you become financially independent.

Now, it's your turn to rewire your brain about the topic of who is responsible for your financial well-being. Below is how I did it.

Limiting Belief: The government and my employer are responsible for my financial well-being.

Personal Truth: When a recession hits or when my employer might pass through some tough financial situation, there is a high probability I might lose my job. If not well prepared, I will not be able to sustain my current lifestyle.

Empowering Belief: I alone am responsible for my well-being. I will learn how to invest in income-producing assets to generate unearned income that will work hard to improve my financial well-being.

Chapter Seven

Limiting Belief: Failure is Bad, and Mistakes are a Reflection of my Incompetence

A COMMON THREAD IS often revealed when I coach business people and investors to overcome a certain challenge in their business. This thread goes along the lines of the fear of failure, rejection, or not being enough—fear is common in our lives. And if we surrender to it, fear can keep us stuck in our comfort zone and prevent us from reaching our true potential. Accepting to live in fear causes a double challenge where you're unfulfilled with the status quo yet afraid to pursue bigger plans in your life.

But fear could also become a blessing to a life free from fear. I know that sounds strange, so let me explain.

If we allow fear to help us break through frustrations and achieve the life we truly desire, it can serve a valuable purpose. That's right, fear can become a tool for finding fulfillment. Discover how to stop living in fear—or use fear as your ultimate inspiration.

Fear and anxiety are powerful sensations that go a long way in keeping us safe. If the dog down the street bites you, the fear that results when you next see this same dog will help you avoid another bite. But what about when the response goes too far? If you instead come to fear all dogs, not just the one that bit you, that fear might drastically change how you act, becoming a detriment, not a benefit.

To stop living in fear, you must understand the underlying psychology so that you can actively work against it. To a point, fear and anxiety have a place in healthy human psychology. Acute fear is a normal emotion that signals a potential threat to your physical or emotional safety. It is a natural response to our survival.

However, when the acute fear response becomes hypersensitive, it becomes chronic fear, which occurs when continually exposed to low-level yet stressful events. Things like the news, pandemics, economic downturns, or workplace challenges irrationally cause us to anticipate negative events. Unlike acute fear, chronic fear can lower our natural life-saving response and cause us to believe we need to be "saved" by an outside force.

Everyone has experienced an anxiety disorder in their lives due to acute fear, irrespective of whether acute or chronic fear. It's typically chronic fear that causes our deep-seated anxiety issues, and everything from the media to our way of life has been blamed. But living in a state of blame has never helped anyone solve their problems. It's time to take ownership of your emotions and transform your life.

"Life is found in the dance between
your deepest desire and your greatest
fear." - Tony Robbins.

The interesting part of the story is that many people go through life without realizing they're living in fear. Please take a moment to ponder this!

That's because fear is often confused with comfort. We become comfortable with our lives and think we are happy and fulfilled with this feeling of certainty. The caveat is when we become too comfortable, it starts to hold us back.

Here are a few signs you are living in fear:

- **Perfectionism** refers to self-defeating thoughts and behaviors aimed at reaching excessively high, unrealistic goals. This need to be or appear perfect, or even to believe that it's possible to achieve perfection, is a mask we wear to protect ourselves from taking action.

- On the other hand, **settling for less** than you deserve is a powerful indicator you're letting your need for certainty run your life. If you don't have passion for your relationship and your job, it's a sign you're living in fear.

- **Procrastinating** and putting off your goals until you have more time is a classic delay tactic for those living in fear. It's time to stop making excuses and start achieving your dreams.

With chronic fear, you're living in a constant state of anxiety. Your fear response influences everything you think, feel, and do, which keeps you stuck in a self-perpetuating cycle of defeat and frustration. The upside to fear is that the emotions surrounding it are usually so unpleasant that they drive you to find another way.

Strategies on How to Stop Living in Fear

Self-care, exercise, and professional help are strategies for stopping fear. Committing to facing your fears will help you discover the strategies that work for overcoming them and finding peace.

1. Determine The Source of Your Anxiety

If you're living in fear, you've reached a point where you're thinking about your worries around the clock without much mindfulness as to what's causing them. To stop living in fear, you must pinpoint what's causing your distress.

Here's an exercise to help you determine the source of your anxiety:

- Get out a piece or open the notes on your device and brainstorm a list. Just write or type down whatever comes to your mind.

- When you're finished, circle the tangible concerns—fears that you'll divorce, lose your house due to foreclosure, or lose your job tomorrow.

- Write down a few actions you can take to prevent these things from happening and start feeling in control.

- Examine the non-circled items, which are the intangible concerns

– things like fears of the apocalypse, alien invasion, and death of humans due to a pandemic. You'll see these have very little chance of happening and are beyond your control. If your fears fall into this category, you must self-reflect to discover how to stop living in fear.

2. Stop The Blame Game

As Tony Robbins says, *"Life doesn't happen to you; it happens for you."*

Truly understanding and accepting this concept is the first step to fulfillment. When you start becoming the master of your destiny, endless possibilities open up to you. In parallel, when you see the world as a place of opportunity, not obstacles, you don't let fear control you.

The reason for determining the source of your anxiety is to help you assert power over those fears so that they no longer control you. You become in the driver's seat.

Once you identify the source, you can change the story that goes in your mind and change your mindset. The first step is recognizing that you have a choice. You can blame outside forces for your emotions and feel out of control or take charge of your life and learn how to stop living in fear.

3. Stop The Excuses

Like blame, excuses are a defense mechanism we use to avoid facing our problems. It's easy to push our hopes, desires, and dreams aside when we have excuses for not having time, money, power, connections, or being too busy. We start to hide behind those excuses instead of taking action to move forward.

Excuses are comforting when we're living in fear. It feels safe to use those excuses against our need to take action. But excuses will also bring you back to exactly where you started. Remember that the next time you fall back on fear and choose to be comfortable instead of facing a challenge, ask yourself whether you're truly where you want to be. You have to learn how to dismiss your easy way out of resorting to excuses.

4. Turn Your "Shoulds" Into "Musts"

If you decide that you have no choice but to succeed, nothing else matters. You'll do whatever it takes to make it happen without leaving room for excuses.

Even the most successful and accomplished people sometimes live in fear. The difference is that rather than allowing fear to suck the life right out of their dreams, they know that the price they will pay if they achieve their goals is far scarier. They know the real fear is living where they have settled or compromised what they wanted.

How do you adopt that mindset and perspective?

Imagine your 80-year-old self sitting in your chair and reflecting on how you lived your life. Look back on your life as if you had not achieved the goal you are after. How has this affected the course of your life? What are your regrets? What do you wish you had made more time for? What do you wish you had attempted? Is there sadness and regret? Are you wondering, "What if. . .?" This way, you can use fear to propel you toward your ultimate goal.

5. Adopt a Growth Mindset

People often give up on what they want because they don't believe in their abilities to reach their goals. They continue living in fear and settling into their current realities, thinking their goal is unattainable, so they don't even try anything. However, the most successful people have adopted a growth mindset, which means they believe in developing their skills and improving their abilities in the face of setbacks. They keep on working harder and developing themselves to challenge those setbacks until they find new strategies to get them to a solution for their problem. They don't give up when things become challenging. Instead, they find new ways to adapt and work harder to achieve their goals.

6. Celebrate the Opportunity of Failure

If you listen to the stories of successful and high achievers, there isn't one successful person in the world who hasn't had to overcome major obstacles. The most painful experiences can bring valuable insights into what you want and don't want in life—what works and doesn't. Failure, disappointment, hiccups, setbacks, challenges, dead-ends—these can all be used to reflect and say, "This didn't work. It wasn't the right fit. So what do I really want?"

In its simplest explanation, we are built to adapt. If you keep this in mind, you can embrace your inner strength and use each experience to help you learn more about yourself and what you must have in life. When you're facing a painful experience or feel ready to give in to fear, picture someone you admire who faced adversity – they wouldn't have achieved the success they now have without learning how to stop living in fear.

You must accept one truth: Failure is inevitable – You will fail. It's just part of becoming successful. Failure provides insights and inherently corrects the faulty ways of approaching a problem. There is no better teacher than the sting of failure. If you use this experience as unique information and adjust your strategy and approach the next time, you will have an advantage that no one else does.

7. Practice Physical and Mental Self-Care

Mental and physical health are fundamentally linked. Multiple associations exist between mental health and chronic physical conditions that significantly impact people's quality of life. The World Health Organization (WHO) defines health as a state of complete physical, mental, and social well-being and not merely the absence of disease or infirmity. In short, there is no health without mental health, and people with chronic physical conditions are at risk of developing poor mental health.

Now that we understand the links between mind and body, the next time you feel like you're living in fear, start with a simple tactic of changing your posture and adopting a "power pose." It can make you feel more confident and less fearful. Physical activity is proven to reduce depression and anxiety, so next time you feel fear coming on, get out and go for a walk, and practice a hobby that keeps your body active. Even better, make exercising a habit, and your mind is set to stay in positive shape. When you combine physical and psychological self-care, you have the recipe to stop living in fear.

Remember that fear cannot coexist with positive emotions—it's either one or the other. You cannot feel both scared and joyful or afraid and grateful, but you can replace one with the other. When you are grateful, fear disappears, and abundance appears. You shift your focus from the negative to the positive. Where focus goes, energy flows, so when you change your mindset this way, you naturally bring more positivity – and less fear – into your life.

8. *Start Living Instead of Worrying*

When living in fear, we often dwell on the past or future. We let our past experiences haunt us and affect our future decisions. We worry so much about what could happen that we forget to enjoy what is happening.

Stop missing your life. Be fully present, practice a new sport or game, and make new acquaintances. Live in the "Now."

If you're ready to learn how to stop living in fear, you must decide that your dreams are more important than your fear of failure. Make the decision today to master your fears and start existing as the most joyful, successful version of yourself possible.

Most of us fear failure and mistakes, which is no surprise. Throughout our years at school and university, failing an exam resulted in a feeling of shame and incompetence. Even in most of our lives as employees, failure to deliver on our objectives will eventually lead to a bad performance evaluation. In extreme cases, the door will be wide open for us to leave our jobs.

Some mature companies accept failure as part of the learning curve of their employees, but those failures need never be experienced more than once, and they should not lead to a major financial loss. In other words, those mature companies are projecting an image of a culture that welcomes failure as part of a learning organization. But when the shit hits the fan, the employee who made a mistake will be looking for a new job in a new company sooner rather than later.

In my professional life as an employee, I used to fear making large mistakes. However, in my professional life as an investor, I have made rather large mistakes and realized that failure is an integral part of my success.

*When I learned how to convert "fear of failure"
into "opportunity of failure", I developed creativity,
flexibility, agility, and the ability to explore new
ways of achieving my goals.*

The biggest mistakes I have made in my investment life have taught me lessons not only about how to avoid them in the future. The solutions to those mistakes have taught me more important lessons about how my "how-to can become more rigid and deliver better results.

When you fail in an important endeavor, you affiliate yourself with some of the most famous people in the world. I am confident you know two famous quotes from Thomas A. Edison, America's greatest inventor. One quote is "I have not failed. I've just found ten thousand ways that won't work", and the other one goes "Many of life's failures are people who did not realize how close they were to success when they gave up". The story's moral is that you fail only when you give up.

Another impressive story is that of Abraham Lincoln, who served as the sixteenth president of the United States. After facing several failures, such as losing his job, failing in business, having a nervous breakdown, being defeated for speaker of the house, being defeated for nomination in Congress, being defeated for the US Senate, and being defeated for nomination for vice president, he overcame each of them as it was time for a better outcome, and was eventually elected president. He is famous for saying, "Always bear in mind that your resolution to succeed is more important than any other." Those great achievers taught us that determination for success will keep us going and trying again and again until we succeed. Who we become in the process becomes as important as success itself.

In summary, I encourage you to start "learning to learn" by "learning to unlearn" false beliefs to move toward success.

Limiting Belief: Failure is bad, and mistakes are a reflection of my incompetence.

Personal Truth: I am worried that people will think I am incompetent if I make mistakes. I would rather be on the safe side and avoid exploring untapped opportunities. But how can I expect different results if I keep doing the same things over and over?

Empowering Belief: Failure is an integral part of my success. Opportunities are always found when I overcome my failures. I become a better person in the process.

Chapter Eight

Limiting Belief: It Takes Money to Make Money

"IT TAKES MONEY TO make money" is a saying older than our grandparents. And as an entrepreneur or investor, you've likely heard it repeatedly. But is it true that it takes money to make money?

The short answer is "Yes," but the real answer is "It takes money to make money, but who said it has to be your money?"

Launching any business venture or investing in any asset takes some money. And if it's a sound business idea or a smart investment, you will find it easy to have others chase you to lend you money or partner with you in return for profit or equity in your business. The idea here is that money follows sound investments.

Turn Your Hobby Into a Money-Making Machine

We live in a "monetize everything you can" culture, where a hobby can become a side hustle that makes some money and potentially turns into a million-dollar enterprise. This means you can start working for yourself to turn fun endeavors into a money-making machine. Over time, you will improve your skills and develop systems to scale up your services to serve more clients, allowing you to turn your gig into a money-making empire. At this point in your career, you'll find yourself in a position where others want to invest in your business for equity. Their capital will help you scale up your business and grow it to new heights while they benefit from their shares in the business growing in value.

Invest in Assets That Create Wealth Using OPM

If you choose to invest in assets that will, in turn, pay you income and build your wealth, you will find many lenders willing to line up and lend you the capital you need to fund your investments. And if you know how to use debt wisely, specifically good debt, you will understand this truth: "The road to wealth is good debt." Returns can reach high double digits only through the wise use of good debt. In the best scenario—when you don't use a single dollar from your own money to purchase income-producing assets—your returns can be infinite. To make it more concrete, if you want to invest in rental properties, a large amount of money is required. Most of us limit ourselves with thoughts such as: "I can never save that amount of money!" so we spend our hard-earned money on discretionary expenses. You can invest in rental properties using other peoples' money (in most cases, the bank's money), and you can borrow anywhere from 80% up to 100% of the property purchase price to own it. I'm sure you've heard of many people around you who purchased properties with zero from their capital.

I invite you to rewire your brain about this limiting belief in money and investing. Although much money is required for investment, who said it has to be my money?

In the chapter on limiting belief number 2, I shared a life-changing lesson: "***The road to wealth is good debt***. " This chapter has explained in depth the principles of borrowing and leverage to create wealth. Returns can reach high double digits only through the wise use of good debt. In the best scenario—when you don't use a single dollar from your own money to purchase income-producing assets—your returns can be infinite.

Let's take rental properties, for example. When you consider investing in income-producing assets, a large amount of money is required. Most of us limit ourselves with thoughts such as, "I can never save that amount of money!" so we spend our hard-earned money on discretionary expenses.

Returns can reach high double digits only through the wise use of good debt. In the best scenario—when you don't use a single dollar from your own money to purchase income-producing assets—your returns can be infinite.

I invite you to transform this limiting belief into an empowering one: "Indeed, it takes money to make money, but who said it has to be my money?"

With this thought, you will start to embrace ideas such as "the road to wealth is good debt" and "I will become as rich as the amount of good debt I take in my life."

I invite you to begin managing your expenses to save money, eventually invest it, and use leverage to accelerate your returns on investment.

The free eBook I am offering you because you are reading this book covers the basics of personal finance. *The Four Stages of Building Wealth* became an international best-seller due to its simplicity and practicality. If you haven't yet downloaded your copy, you can do so by visiting www.employeemillionaire.com/the4stages.

It's your turn now to rewrite your belief about money and investing.

Limiting Belief: It takes money to make money.

Personal Truth: A large amount of money is required for investment. I can never save that amount of money. I, therefore, end up spending my hard-earned money on discretionary expenses.

Empowering Belief: Indeed, it takes money to make money, but who said it has to be my money? The road to wealth is good debt. I will become as rich as the amount of good debt I take in my life. I will not need more than 20% of my own money to invest in rental properties, so I shall begin managing my expenses to save money and eventually invest it and use leverage to accelerate my returns on investment.

Chapter Nine

Limiting Belief: Investing is Complicated and Risky. Others Can Manage My Money More Wisely

As of the writing of this book, more than 30,000 students have taken our personal finance and real estate courses. We've engaged with hundreds of our students and learned that most used to believe that investing was complicated and risky.

They eventually ended up depending on their earned income and waking up one day when their income went lower, or they saw themselves out of a job. To me, this is risky. It is riskier to keep depending on your job until you face the reality of diminishing income or losing all your earned income later in life.

Some of our students have sought the help of professional financial advisors to invest their money and then learned that those advisors rarely put their client's interests before their own. Those advisors get paid regardless of whether their clients make or lose money.

Financial advisors are employees, agents, or brokers for financial institutions. They earn their income by selling investments to their clients. They are interested in generating high returns for their clients, but I don't believe they will place their customers' interests before their own.

I am trying to say that although those financial advisors might be looking after your money, you owe it to yourself to become actively engaged in your financial planning. Higher returns are more secure when you become involved in the decisions on how and where to invest your money. You do not want to be another proof of the old saying, "A fool and his money are soon parted." In the extreme case of losing your money because of bad advice, you can rest assured that your financial advisor has already received payment or commission for the advice given to you. The advisor wins in either case, whether you win or lose.

Investment is not as risky as it might appear. It is less risky than having a job, which you might lose sooner or later. I am not saying there is no risk associated with an investment. Great investors minimize risk by following sound investment principles and proven models. You may have heard that investors make their money going in. This suggests that smart investors buy assets with more value than the tag price. It means they are sure that their profit has been made when going in since they bought the asset at a discount compared to the market price.

I want to share a personal story illustrating how investors make money. In 2010, I moved to live in Dubai. The country was still experiencing the aftermath of the 2008 recession when the stock and real estate markets plummeted. In a certain prime area, where all ex-pats looked for places to live, the average price of a two-bedroom townhouse had dropped from $762,000 before 2008 to an average of $448,000 in 2010. Very few people, if any, were buying properties during this period.

When I shared with my friends and colleagues that I was planning to buy a property, they all thought I was crazy, inviting risk into my door. Warren Buffet once said: "The time to get interested is when no one else is. You can't buy what is popular and do well." Following that advice and my understanding of the market that there was a higher demand for rent since no one was buying properties, I decided to search for a property that was around 20% below the already-depressed market value.

I contacted the bank and got a home loan preapproval. I then searched online for property listings. I found out about five active agents I managed to contact and eventually meet. When they knew how serious I was, they started searching the market for properties marked lower than the market price. One day, one of the agents called to inform me that he had found a two-bedroom townhouse for sale for $355,000. This was more than my 20% discount criterion. Without a second thought, I issued an offer letter with a promise of a 10% down payment, subject to the seller's approval of my offer. The seller needed to sell since he was kicked out of his job and planned to travel back to the UK in a few weeks. We signed a contract and closed the deal in less than three weeks. At that time, I could have resold the property for market price and easily made a $93,000 profit if I put the property back on the market. The only advantage I had over the previous owner was time. I had the privilege of having time to wait for the property to get sold, whereas he was working on a tight schedule and had to leave the country in less than two months.

So, by buying the property at a discounted price, I minimized the risk or even removed the risk from the equation. The interesting part of this investment was that the bank had agreed to lend me 80 percent of the appraised property value. The property was appraised close to market value, to be exact, at $430,000. The 80% loan-to-value (LTV) was equivalent to $344,000. The total closing cost, including a 4% closing fee, was $369,200 ($355,000 + $14,200). The amount paid from my pocket was only $25,200 ($369,200 - $344,000).

Figure 12—An example of purchasing below market price and investing little from the investor's own capital

Then, after transferring the title into my name, I lined up a tenant to rent the property from day one. The annual rent was $24,500. The annual mortgage payment was $19,704 ($1,642 monthly × 12 months). The annual association and maintenance fees were $2,177. Accordingly, the net cash flow was $2,619 ($24,500 - $19,704 - $2,177). This is equivalent to a 10.4% ROI on my invested capital of $25,200.

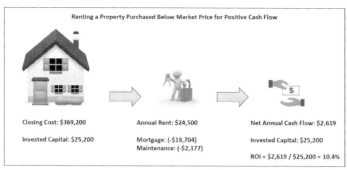

Figure 13—Renting a property purchased below market price for positive cash flow

The market in Dubai started gaining momentum in 2012, and I sold the property in 2015 for $639,500 with a capital gain of $270,300, equivalent to 1,072 percent ROI on my invested capital of $25,200.

At the time I bought this property, many colleagues challenged me, saying that if the market dropped further, I would lose all my invested capital and still must pay the bank for the amount of the loss. I knew a loss would be actualized only if I sold the property at a loss. Otherwise, it was all paper loss. So, with the strategic intent of renting out the house, even with no future rent increases, at 10.4 percent ROI, I would have returned my invested capital in 9.6 years. The worst-case scenario was still much better than any interest I might get from any bank or financial institution.

Figure 14—Risk management in rental property invest-ment

The example above illustrates risk management. I have planned for rental income with steady income at 10.4 percent ROI as the worst-case scenario, and I would have been happy if I achieved only 10.4 percent ROI. It beats any interest I might earn in stashing my money into a savings account. However, when the opportunity for a huge capital gain presented itself due to market cycles, I took advantage of it and sold at 1,072 percent ROI.

Most people make the mistake of planning for capital gain only without calculating the rental income as a cushion to fall on if the market does not go as they wish or as well-spoken financial advisors or real estate agents promised.

Many of my friends and colleagues who challenged and warned me meant my best. Almost everyone had a bad experience or a friend or relative who lost their shirt in the 2008 recession. With my curiosity to understand why they lost their investments, it appeared that their negative experiences all revolved around buying a property off-plan with a promise of capital gain in three to four years when it would be handed over to them. So, those investors were planning only for capital gains. They couldn't plan for rentals since those property purchases were off-plan.

When the recession hit in 2008, those investors saw the prices of their properties, which were still plans on paper, plummet by almost half. The developers either went bankrupt or demanded continuous payments from those investors on the contract price. Many of those investors chose to let go of their paid money, dropped their investments, and eventually lost it all. This is the opposite case of risk management. This is risk mismanagement. Those who lost such investments were all in a challenging situation. They couldn't justify paying for lost value properties, which could not generate cash flow. I wish people would learn from such mistakes.

After the market started growing again in Dubai, the developers and their brilliant talkative agents managed to convince people to buy properties off-plan and that, this time, the market wouldn't go into recession again. I wonder how those agents can read the future. I would pay millions to buy a crystal ball that could predict the future.

One of my closest friends, whom I greatly respect, is a well-established business owner who found himself having too much money and not knowing where to invest it. No wonder real estate agents, like wolves, will lay their eyes on prey with too much meat and fat. They convinced my friend to buy off-plan properties in an area that was not yet developed. This area was still a desert. They showed him attractive animated videos and brochures of what the development would look like when it was finished in three or four years. They showed him simulations of how he would more than double his money in three or four years. The dream of fast and easy money thoroughly tricked him, and he signed the contract and made a down payment without consulting anyone.

On the same day, he called me, asking me to congratulate him on his new investment, which he was so proud of. He tried to convince me that his agent had saved a few other properties for some elite clients and that he could convince his agent to keep a unit for me to invest in.

Not wanting him to feel regret, I wished him good luck and explained my investment method and criteria. I also offered my future help in case he would like an opinion.

Less than two months later, he signed a similar off-plan deal for a million dollars, promising to double this investment in four years. I wish him good luck and hope those agents do have a crystal ball and that he will double his money. The agent was paid his commission regardless of whether the property appreciated or depreciated in four years.

I recommend planning for the risks and opportunities for every investment you plan to make. It would be best if you were content with the outcome of the risk. The fear and risk of failure will always be in front of you. It is normal. The way you handle fear determines the results you will have in life. If you are equipped with the knowledge, you can overcome fear. Otherwise, the lack of knowledge only makes you submit to it. Knowledge causes fear to disappear. I encourage you to read about successful people and to seek mentors and coaches in your life. This book is intended to equip you with the knowledge I have accumulated over the years from my failures and successes in real estate investment, the books I have read, and the seminars I have attended.

In his book, The Top 10 Distinctions Between Millionaires and the Middle Class, Keith Cameron Smith shares an empowering way to look at risks and opportunities in every investment. He recommends asking ourselves three questions:

- What's the worst thing that could happen?

- What's the best thing that could happen?

- What's the most likely thing that might happen?

After answering those questions, reflect on them. If you can live with the worst thing that could happen, and if the most likely thing that may happen will get you closer to your goals, then go for it.

Limiting Belief: Investing is complicated and risky. Others can manage my money more wisely.

Personal Truth: I am lazy. I do not want to take responsibility for my finances. I will seek the help of professionals who can manage my money.

Empowering Belief: Investment is as complicated as I think it is. With proven methods, I can be in control of my investments. I will manage risk and take advantage of opportunities.

The only way out of the rat race is to take risks. If I take the risk out of life, I take the opportunity out of life.

Chapter Ten
Limiting Belief: Successful Investors Have a Crystal Ball That Enables Them to Time the Market

IN THE PREVIOUS LIMITING belief about investment and risk, I explained how wise investors invest with clear criteria and plan for worst-case scenarios. Once they are in the game, whenever opportunities present themselves, they will act upon them and achieve high returns. For an outsider, the image is different. People hold the mistaken belief that successful investors really can time the market. They do not understand that those investors were already in the market and then took advantage of opportunities.

Between 2010 and 2012, I bought three townhouses, intending to rent them out for cash flow. I managed my risk and bought properties that were more than 20 percent less than the market price. With the right buying price, I made my profit going in. The net cash flow from renting out those three properties was positive, with ROIs ranging between 10 to 17 percent. I was quite happy with such returns.

When the market in Dubai started to regain its 2008 losses and even started to get irrationally high, I took advantage of this window of opportunity. I sold those three properties in 2015 with a total profit of over a million dollars. All those agents and bankers I was working with to acquire those properties believed that I had a crystal ball and could time the market. I consistently explained to them that I purchased those properties for the cash flow. Still, I saw an enormous capital gain opportunity when the market ticked up in 2015, so I immediately sold them for a handsome profit.

The funny part of the story is that my friends and colleagues who thought I was stupid to invest in properties in 2010 all thought I was smart in 2015. The fact of the matter is that I am neither stupid nor smart. I am just an investor with clear criteria and objectives who had a stake in the market when it changed course and started to grow again at a very high pace.

After a strong comeback in 2015, the market in Dubai softened a bit. I immediately bought a couple of properties. The banker I always work with to get loans still calls me every couple of weeks for advice on how the market is going. Every time, I tell him that I don't know. I don't think he believes me since I still receive those calls. To be transparent, I am enjoying those calls more than he is because I always ask him about the number of home loans the bank is granting. I am getting data from him that will enable me to understand where the market might be going. Please note that I said "might." I never convince myself that whatever data I read will tell me what will happen next or when.

In other instances, some of the agents I frequently work with also call me to ask about when the market will drop or improve. I tell them, too, that I don't know. Given the frequency of calls I receive from the same agents in a short period, I feel they do not believe me either.

Most people think timing the market is about sitting on the sidelines and actively observing until they identify the golden moment to jump in and make a fortune. They don't understand that timing is about always being in the game, then, when opportunities show up, taking advantage of them. In other words, timing is not about being in the right place at the right time; it's about always being in that place and then leveraging any opportunity.

Warren Buffet once said: "We have long felt that the only value of stock forecasters is to make fortune-tellers look good." I'm amazed at how many investors take market forecasters seriously, even when they have no credible track records of success. Warren Buffet also advises against trying to predict the direction of the stock market, the economy, interest rates, or elections.

I hope you agree with me that no one has a crystal ball to time the market. What is your new set of beliefs about timing the market?

Limiting Belief: Successful investors have a crystal ball that enables them to time the market.

Personal Truth: My fear and laziness made me believe timing the market is about sitting on the sidelines and actively observing until I identify the golden moment to jump in and make a fortune.

Empowering Belief: Timing is about always being in the game. Then, when opportunities show up, I can take advantage of them.

Chapter Eleven

Limiting Belief: Investors Have Specific Knowledge That Most People Cannot Have

INVESTMENT INDEED REQUIRES SOME education and research on the part of the investor. Warren Buffet recommended that investors never invest in a business they cannot understand. He added, "What counts for most people in investing is not how much they know, but how realistically they define what they don't know." In other words, investing in what you don't know or understand cannot be classified as investing. Investing in something you do not understand is pretty much like gambling.

A good example is my friend, who bought two expensive properties off-plan by following the advice of an agent who said he would more than double his money in four years. My friend is counting on luck, and I really do wish him all the luck.

Real investment is investing in what you know and fully understand. Suppose you do not have a deep understanding of any specific area. In that case, I encourage you to look for a topic that greatly interests you and commit to studying and researching it to become an expert over time.

If real estate is an area you want to educate yourself on, my program – *The Employee to Millionaire Real Estate Investor Course* – becomes quite handy in your journey. Check it out at www.employeemilliona ire.com/vcp.

Do you still believe that investors have specific knowledge that others cannot have?

Limiting Belief: Investors have specific knowledge that most people cannot have.

Personal Truth: My arrogance, ignorance, and laziness made me believe I have an idea about investment and that I am not up to it.

Empowering Belief: Real investment is investing in what I know and fully understand. I commit to studying an area of investment to become an expert in it over time.

Chapter Twelve

Limiting Belief: Investors Diversify Their Investments to Minimize Risk

"DIVERSIFY YOUR INVESTMENTS" IS the most common advice financial advisors offer. Why do you think Warren Buffet believes otherwise when he said, "Diversification is a protection against ignorance"?

He also said that concentrating on only a few holdings can greatly reduce risk. This precious advice suggests that investors become deeply knowledgeable in an investment area and then stick to what they know.

It is like putting all your eggs in one basket and then watching over this basket. Think of it as a kind of protection. We cannot possibly understand all the moving parts of the economy and the countless investment choices available to us, but we can focus and become experts in one or a few types of investments. In that way, we minimize risk.

In *The Employee to Millionaire Real Estate Investor* program, all the how-to of real estate investments will be shared with you. What you will be learning is a wealth of information I have assimilated from many books, seminars, webinars, coaching from real estate advisors, and my personal experience. I am trying to simplify it with video illustrations to improve the chances that anyone can understand and then apply the learning. Check it out at www.employeemillionaire.com/vcp.

Here is how I rewired my brain on the topic of diversification.

Limiting Belief: Investors diversify their investments to minimize risk.

Personal Truth: When I do not know which investments will deliver the best returns on my invested capital, I will diversify to protect myself against ignorance.

Empowering Belief: I plan to become knowledgeable in an area of investment and then stick to what I know.

Chapter Thirteen

Limiting Belief: All Good Investments are Taken. Only Mediocre and Bad Investments are Left Over to Small Investors

MOST UNKNOWLEDGEABLE PEOPLE ARE cynical about investment. They often claim that all good investments are taken and that only mediocre and bad investments are left over for small investors. Savvy investors wouldn't miss opportunities to make good investments. Why can't you join the league of those investors?

The marketplace is dynamic, with economic and personal forces always at work, generating a continuous flow of investment opportunities.

Economic forces such as interest rates, employment rates, population growth, population shifts, and area developments have a major impact on the market. As a result, the prices of properties might be driven up or down. Such economic forces are big and are on the news to the extent that they may often mask the impact of personal forces in putting opportunities in the market.

For example, personal situations like marriage, divorce, an increase in household size, relocation, death, inability to pay a mortgage, and family disputes over inheritance all present opportunities in the market. Those personal forces present more opportunities at discounted prices just because those people want to get rid of a property for personal reasons sooner rather than later. Such personal factors have always been there and will always remain there.

Do you still believe opportunities at a bargain price tag are all taken?

Limiting Belief: All the good investments are taken. Only mediocre and bad investments are left over to small investors.

Personal Truth: I am lazy about searching for opportunities. If I create the excuse that all opportunities are taken, I will feel better about my inaction.

Empowering Belief: Opportunities are in the market every day. If I am in the game, opportunities will eventually present themselves for me to take advantage of them.

Chapter Fourteen
Motivated Money Mindset That Helps

HAVING READ THE LIMITING beliefs explained in this book, I am confident you've concluded that accumulating wealth and achieving financial independence depends on your money mindset.

The truth is everyone struggles with one financial challenge or the other. Regardless of how little you earn or how huge your income is, no one is above a financial challenge. How you train your mind to react to a financial situation is very significant.

However, most people attempt to tackle their financial situations severely logically and get so hard on themselves when savings and budgeting efforts fail. Without a doubt, when dealing with financial struggles, it often comes down to numbers, yet applying certain habits and behavioral patterns to back those mathematical solutions necessitates that we look at other factors that shape our financial lives, including our emotions, point of view, and the overall illogicality that combine to make us human.

Experiencing a financial challenge can be frustrating, particularly if you've repeatedly been battling the same issue. So, it would be best to change your money mindset from a poverty-driven mindset to an abundance-driven one. This is not difficult to achieve if you know just what to do. If you've been struggling financially, here are some tested formulas you can implement to tackle your financial situation and bounce back financially.

But before we do that, let's define your "money mindset." It's the prevailing attitude you have regarding your finances that motivates your key financial decisions. The money mindset is our unique attitude and perspective about money and ourselves. Our mindset about money affects our money relationship and the outcomes we realize. The reason is that the way we think about a thing informs how we interact with it and the actions we take concerning it.

The way we view money shapes our attitude toward others, whether they are poor or rich. For instance, if you believe that rich people are evil, materialistic, greedy, pompous, and awfully mean, so you don't want to associate with them. Then, this will affect your ability to make money. Similarly, if you believe being poor makes you virtuous and noble, you like poor people. This will hinder your ability and motivation to make money.

Your responses and reactions during financial conversations indicate your money mindset. Do you believe that only the male population should make money? Do you feel confident, in control, or vulnerable and uncomfortable during a financial discussion?

When used correctly, the human mind is powerful and compels certain things to change in our lives. If you adopt a mindset, you can make better decisions about dealing with your struggle. According to Fitz Gilbert, we are what we think, and having the right attitude toward our finances will positively and directly impact our financial situations and how we overcome those challenges.

The following are proven steps to help you adopt a motivated and positive money mindset. They are easy to implement.

Understand What Money Means to You

The first question to ask yourself is: Why do I want to make money? Knowing your motivation can help your financial situation. Are you afraid of being broke? Do you want to make money to climb up the social ladder? You need to assess what motivates your money decisions. Is it fear that you'll go broke if you don't save more? Or are you inspired by the rewards that come with making money?

Several factors aside, just thinking about money increases cash flow into your bank account and your hands. To combat your financial situation, you must understand what money means to you. It would be best if you milked whatever inspires you to make money; that way, you can be reinforced to keep pursuing your financial aspirations.

Recognize That No Financial Challenge is Unfixable

Recognize that there is no insurmountable hurdle anywhere. Every financial challenge has a solution. Just because you haven't figured it out does not mean the solution is not out yet; it does not mean you won't eventually.

Stop focusing on the enormity of the challenge or what's wrong, or you won't be motivated to seek solutions. Instead, start focusing on the benefits of attaining financial independence, living a stress-free life, accumulating wealth, and how you can spend your money on things you need, want, or towards a bigger purpose of helping people around you and the community you live in. It's much easier to stay motivated and achieve all your financial goals when you maintain a positive outlook.

Change Your Money Outlook

It is easy to feel down and depressed when everything is not going the way you want it to. Be positive that everything will work out, and keep on trying. Accept that the small steps you've taken thus far add to the progress. You are solely responsible for your reactions. A positive money mindset will help you be more productive and develop a better relationship with money.

Sometimes, you need a break to refuel when you can't make head or tail of your finances. Worry has yet to change any situation. You may have to go out with your friends or loved ones, go to the cinema, or practice a hobby.

Making Room for Gratitude Can Determine Your Altitude

I want to ask you a question, "Are you grateful?"

Almost every one of us, deep in our hearts, will respond, "Yes! I'm very grateful for everything God has done for me!"

If my question is tweaked, I would like to ask you to reflect on your answer, "Are you still as grateful in the tough times?"

I bet you will take some time to think about that question. After some soul search, many might respond, "Well, no."

If we're honest with ourselves, gratitude doesn't always come naturally, particularly when we experience tough times.

When the COVID-19 pandemic hit the world like a tsunami, almost every family experienced a family member hit with the disease, and their first response was not "Thank you, Lord."

If you lost your job in the 2008 global financial crisis or the 2020 pandemic, I am sure you didn't say, "Thank you, Lord! What can I learn from this ordeal?"

When facing tough times, our natural response is to ask questions and feel unrest. However, when we learn to focus on being grateful and not on our problems, we strengthen our faith in the midst of what we face. Only at this stage can we redirect our focus away from our "big problem" to our "better alternative."

Please pause and reflect!

First, as part of this pause, I want to thank you for reading this book. I am grateful to be connected with you through its words.

That's what this "pause" is all about—being thankful and having an Attitude of Gratitude.

We should consciously practice gratitude multiple times daily—to be grateful for the smallest things in our lives. It's yet another way of building inner energy and vitality for our quest for personal development.

I think the healthiest human emotion is "gratitude" because if we learn how to be thankful in the valley, imagine the magnitude of our celebration on the mountaintop." Gratitude is the best attitude that takes us to the next altitude!

Here are powerful concepts, if well practiced, that can transform your attitude from an "Attitude of Self-Absorption" to an "Attitude of Gratitude."

Appreciation: Appreciate everything for what it is (and not for what you would like it to be), and appreciate it "at the moment." That means being thankful for the smallest little things we usually take for granted — our family, friends, health, career, nature, and even those tiny rays of sunshine through the clouds on a stormy day. While it is not usually our default attitude, learning to cherish anything and everything we experience in our daily lives can go a long way toward alleviating our daily problems and challenges. Once we have this inner peace of "appreciation," the magic happens when we get into the habit of expressing our appreciation for such joy to everyone around us. Just imagine the positive energy we will be transferred to people around us.

Approval: Many of us lose energy in the endless process of seeking the approval of others, whereas we should have had the inner peace of feeling good about ourselves without needing anyone else's approval. When we have self-belief, we appreciate, value, and accept ourselves; we have self-confidence. But, when we believe that nothing we do is ever good enough, it takes its toll on our mental and emotional well-being. It can lead to emotional stress. Stop comparing your successes and achievements to others. Stop despairing right now. Remember: you are unique, and you have special qualities. To help you recognize your worth, here are five steps to follow:

1. Get focused on what you are doing right and what you do have instead of what you are doing wrong and what you don't have.

2. Ask a close, trusted friend to help you identify what makes you unique. Just remember, what you do well can be small or large.

3. Stop putting everyone else above you so that you don't end up in an endless quest for the approval of others.

4. Ignore all destructive criticism and make your opinion of yourself the most important one. Do not internalize anything that negative people say about you. Their opinion is just that - an opinion, not a fact.

5. Do not let other people weaken your spirit or ridicule your ambitions. Work on your ambitions, and then let your results speak for themselves.

Once you have mastered self-approval, conveying approval will always pay off — "believing that someone or something is good or acceptable." You can start by making a mental list of those whose contributions to your life you value and then openly express it to them. Just imagine the positive impact you will make in their lives!

Admiration: Expressing admiration is like the next level of appreciating others. It is about being generous with your praise for all the great things around you. A simple gesture of paying simple compliments to everyone you think deserves them — from the waiter who served your meal to the janitor cleaning the office, to the barista preparing your coffee, to the person who smiled at you in the elevator, and all your colleagues who make your ability to do your job so much easier. Compliment them and tell them how much you appreciate them and what they do. Look for genuine reasons to compliment people and watch the positive responses you get in return.

Attention: Giving attention in this busy world of distractions could be tough. Let's face it: you try to give your undivided attention to someone talking to you or to this book you are reading, and then you get a notification from your social media, a message on your phone, an ad pops out on your screen, a sales agent calls you or your mind is worried about something else at home or work. We all know that we have to give others the attention they deserve by not only listening to what they are saying but, most importantly, processing that and acknowledging what is being said. There is no greater sign of respect for the other person than listening intently to them and understanding them. Another component of attention is an awareness of all that's happening around you and realizing how the most seemingly unimportant, inconsequential, or trivial things can impact your life, positively or negatively. It can even lead to big opportunities if you show gratitude for them. But to do that, you must pay attention, or you're liable to miss out on them entirely.

We all have challenges. We all have struggles and face hardship at different times in our lives. How we face those unpleasant life situations will impact our lives. We can either allow them to knock us down or positively face them, pick up the pieces, learn from the experience, and move on.

Of course, hard times can be emotionally draining; however, if we reflect on the situation, we can always find the lesson in everything that happens to us (and for us). The question is, are you willing to look for it?

Life is filled with lessons, each allowing us to learn something from it and improve ourselves. When we choose to have an attitude of gratitude and be grateful for even the smallest things, we can change our lives.

> *"An attitude of gratitude will determine the level of altitude at which you are able to soar."* - Tomyka Washington

You become what you think about all the time. If you allow yourself to procrastinate and surrender to the fear of every downfall you will face, the more those negative attitudes become your reality. On the other hand, when you have an attitude of gratitude and can find the positive even during trials, you become available to receive the lessons life wants to teach you.

Living Your "Dash" Will Determine the Legacy You Leave

Early in my career, when I was still in the corporate world, one of the coaches who left a big impact on my life once asked a team of executives: "What is your dash?"

Sitting on the table, we all looked at each other with an exclamation mark on our forehead. I thought it was a trick question.

When he saw me a bit confused between answering him and being hesitant to look stupid, he paused for a few seconds to allow me some time to think and then gave me a hint to imagine what might be written on the tombstone of a person who died.

I immediately concluded that he meant the dash that separates a person's date of birth and date of death, which is the time a person spends alive on earth.

He asked me again: "What is your dash? When your eulogy is read, would you be proud of the things they will say about you and about how you spent your years from birth till death?"

Then, he addressed everyone around him at the table and recommended not answering his question. But he strongly advised us to reflect on our dash and think of anything we want to change in our lives.

I considered this an opportunity for any person to rewrite their dash. With those words, I realized that what matters the most is how we live and love during our years on this earth. It does not matter how much wealth we accumulate for the sake of wealth, but we can think of wealth as an enabler to spend quality time with our loved ones.

What are you cut for? With my coach's help, I clarified my purpose in life: Adding value to people's lives. This became the filter for every decision I make, including writing articles and books. When my coach helped me identify my priorities in life, serving God, my family, and the community were at the top of the list. Everything else became secondary or an enabler. This is exactly how I see creating wealth and having plenty of money—as an enabler. Being wealthy and financially free can offer you choices in life. You can choose to retire early and spend more quality time with your family and serve the community; you can also choose to open a business you have always wanted to venture into, or you can choose to remain employed for a company you enjoy working with, especially if you have reached a senior position and if you love your job. Whatever you choose, being financially free will allow you to have more conviction in your decisions. Gone will be the days when you will be forced to stay in a job you hate!

What are your priorities? Thinking about what your own dash is will always be time well spent. I rarely see people give their lives adequate thought and determine their purpose. On the contrary, I often see people spend ample time planning for their day-to-day things or vacations. Don't get caught up in the daily stuff. You will be better off thinking of your life beyond material things. If you make it a practice to revisit your "Big Why" list every year and often refer to it to remind yourself of it, that would be a great start.

Seek the help of gardeners, not mechanics! It is amazing how a coach can help you figure out the important things you want to achieve and how a mentor can help you achieve those goals. While digging in my notes, I found a simple definition that differentiates a coach from a mentor. "A coach has some great questions for your answers; a mentor has some great answers for your questions." The coaches I had the honor to work with in my life asked me many challenging questions that triggered my thoughts and made me look for answers. In parallel, I have worked with great mentors who have helped me with the answers to the questions triggered by my coaches. On that topic, I reflect on what one of my coaches always talked about in differentiating between the gardener and the mechanic. A gardener creates an environment that nurtures personal growth and allows one to stretch and expand one's mind beyond one's comfort zone. Whereas a mechanic fixes things—or people. How many of us want to be fixed? Not many. Without the help of coaches and mentors, our mistakes could have been plentiful, and we might not have achieved whatever success we have so far in our respective lives. You will need the help of coaches and mentors to guide you on the journey you would select for yourself. You will need someone to hold you accountable for achieving your objectives. You will need someone to help you unfold the priorities you will have down the road a few years from now. You will be amazed how your priorities in life will evolve throughout the years, especially when you grow in experience, skills, and wealth.

You Don't Have To Do It Alone

You don't have to go to it alone. Understand that asking for help does not mean you're weak or a failure. Ask for and accept assistance from others rather than struggling silently.

Seek the help of mentors and coaches, read books and blogs focused on financial education, listen to audiobooks, attend master classes, and get online courses.

A change of attitude isn't all required to change your financial situation. It would be best if you also achieved balance in your financial life. If all you think about is how to live a stress-free life, you may not have savings to fall back on in emergencies. You will not have an effective retirement cushion if you spend all of your time focused on your budget today. So, strive for balance to achieve financial stability.

I invite you to book a call to discuss your money mindset, financial challenges, and ambitions. I'll happily listen, understand your challenges, and guide you toward your ambitions. Consider this call a "thank you" for

reading this book. Whenever you feel you're ready, visit this page: www
.employeemillionaire.com/book-call.

Chapter Fifteen

The Three Money Habits To Overcome Financial Stress

Do you often get absent-minded thinking about money problems throughout the day? What about waking up in the middle of the night anxiously making some mental calculations about paying your bills, rent, mortgage, credit card, and other expenses?

This is when you feel you're in a financial mess, consuming most of your mental energy. It makes you feel like a loser, and it all goes in vicious circles. But you can fight back and emerge as a winner in the money game!

The first step would be to confront reality and clearly understand what's causing your financial stress. So, let's look at common reasons why people think they're slowly sinking into the ocean of debt and bills.

Causes of Financial Stress

If you've been feeling that your financial stress is leading to emotional stress and health complications, you're right. It has been medically proven that financial stress can trigger long-term diseases and emotional stress, which in turn lead to more financial stress.

As with any problem, the first step is acknowledging and analyzing what's causing it. The obvious answer to your financial stress may be around money, but check why money is only the symptom of your problem and not the root cause.

The common manifestations and causes of financial stress are:

- *Expenses are greater than income*: You spend more than you earn. You're maxing out your credit, taking personal loans for trivial things, or starting to withdraw from your retirement fund. The real cause here is your spending habit that turns into an addiction that keeps on going on for a long period until you can't borrow more money, and then you get a big slap on the face.

- *Living paycheck to paycheck*: You spend your paycheck and get left with more days at the end of your money until the next pay-check. Somehow, you manage to survive, and like a drug addict, your next paycheck refreshes you again, and you go into the same cycle every month. You complain that your salary is wiped out by paying off your bills and debt obligations. The real cause, here again, is your spending habit.

- *Debt*: The feeling of paying off debt from a big chunk of your salary makes you feel stuck in the hamster wheel. You feel you're working only to pay back your lender! You often won't remember why you've even taken that debt in the first position. This goes back to your spending habit, where you've taken bad debt to purchase products and services of no real value, and that gave you some instant gratification.

- **Lack of financial plan**: You feel you've lost control of your finances. You sit there on your floater, trying to survive and hoping the wind will take you to a safe shoar one day. Not knowing any better, you might get drowned in the ocean of spending.

Quick Fixes Won't Solve Your Money Stress

You might think having more money solves your problem outright. You start working harder to get your next promotion and that long-awaited pay raise. You get sucked into "Get Rich Quick Schemes," and you lose more money on the false promises of getting rich.

The reality is that the more money we have, the higher our financial stress will be if we continue our bad spending habits. It's human nature to have an insatiable thirst for more things than money can buy.

The real enemy here is us—it's our money and spending habits.

The real key to dealing with financial stress is to change your money habits:

1. Spend smarter,

2. Save some, and

3. Invest in income-producing assets.

Fight Financial Stress With These 3 Money Habits

Now that we've realized we've been standing in our own way to financial success, we need to master the money habits that will help us eliminate financial stress.

1. Spend Smarter

We spend two main types of expenses: essential and discretionary expenses.

While essential expenses are essential for survival, little can be done here. However, it would be wise to check our spending on housing and other essential expenses.

Regarding your discretionary expenses, here is where most of us get trapped. We tend to spend what we have on the things that will get us instant gratification. Even worse, we borrow money (bad debt), using our credit or taking loans to buy things that will not serve us any good for our retirement. We all enjoy spending on expensive dinners, designer clothes, and flashy cars, but those things have to be paid for from another stream of income - not your salary. Indeed, if you're looking for another income source, you can earn extra income while you keep your day job.

2. Save Some

As an automatic consequence of spending smarter, you will be left with more money to save. What to do with this saved money will be covered in the next point below.

Good spending habits tend to lower bad debt. Work out a plan with a financial coach to pay your bad debt, starting with the liabilities with the highest interest rates. Identify unnecessary expenses that you can re-allocate to debt payment. The faster you can pay all your bad debt, the sooner you will switch your financial reality from a financial stress situation to financial comfort.

After paying off your bad debt, you must go on a mission to save at least 10% of your income. You've already acquired the habit of spending smarter and paying off your bad debt. In this next phase, you need to start reallocating the money you've used to pay off your bad debt toward your savings.

Believe that you can solve your money problem. Some people have been in worse financial problems than you, and they can get out of their dilemma. Believe that you still have control over your finances, and you start bringing hope back into your home.

3. Invest in Income-Producing Assets

Now that you've paid off your bad debt and saved at least 10% of your income, it's time to put this money to work for you.

Here's where many of us get lost again!

There are hundreds and hundreds of investing options, but trust me most we don't (and never) have control over. It's like gambling our money on the optimistic promise of future gains.

It has been proven, over the centuries, that investing in income-producing assets is where most of the rich and wealthy have either made or preserved their wealth. We are talking about investing in assets that pay you a steady stream of residual income for as long as you own those assets. Any capital gains come as the cherry on top of the cake.

Some financial coaches or specialists can help people solve their money problems. You can also talk to a family member or close friend and ask for financial assistance if you believe this is in your best interest.

It All Starts With Your Money Habits!

Having more money is not the solution to your financial stress. Changing your money habits is what will help you recover from financial stress.

Is there a bad financial situation that you were able to come out of? How did you do it?

Chapter Sixteen

How Not To Let Your Ambitions and Dreams Break And Sink?

WITHOUT A DOUBT, WE'VE all read (or watched related movies or documentaries) about the disaster that happened in the early morning of 15 April 1912—the sinking of the Titanic!

On that morning, a new page of dark history has been written. This resulted in the deaths of more than 1,500 people! Those were people with families, loved ones, friends, dreams, ambitions,...!

The ship of dreams ended up in complete silence and darkness in the deep waters of the ocean.

Many of us start our career pumped up with dreams and ambitions, and then we hit obstacles and challenges, we surrender, and allow our dreams and ambitions to settle for less... and even sink!

Let me explain why. In today's fast-paced life, we get distracted by hundreds and hundreds of messages every hour. We get sucked into other people's lifestyles and we imagine ourselves living their lives. Most of the time, what we see is "sexy" for social media, but may not be a true reflection of reality. Very few talk about their past (and current) failures and challenges.

We want to enjoy the same life those influencers and gurus are living, but then... hey... we realize their lifestyle is something far beyond our reach. This leads us to stop following our dreams, then procrastinating, and complaining all the time about our life!

We then stop looking for solutions for our today's problems and challenges and hide behind many excuses that we create. We allow our ship to sink into the piles of bills, debt, responsibilities, and negativity around us. Our problem seems endless and we sink deeper and deeper as our credit card loans, personal loans, student loans, and other loans only get bigger and bigger... exactly like the Titanic sank in the cold waters of the Atlantic Ocean.

Time passes by... and then we refresh ourselves... trying to stay afloat and then see a glimpse of hope and get energized again to live amazing lives and do extraordinary things. Our problems are pulling us down on one hand, but our dreams and ambitions are lifting us.

One of those two forces will win!

If we keep on doing what we've been doing, then most probably we will be facing a similar fate like the titanic.

If we act on our dreams and ambitions... by taking small baby steps... the odds are our ship will float and sail toward those dreams and ambitions.

When Is The Time To Act?

Time is your worst enemy and your best friend, don't forget that time won't ever come back again.

It's your decision whether you start living the life you want and provide for your children a better future.

You decide whether you want to become a Titanic or start living the life you were created to live!

You might feel like you need a miracle in your life right now.

You don't need miracles! You're alive and that's the biggest miracle you can ever get, now get to work, because dreams won't become reality without taking action!

You would like to start but you don't how, or where, you don't have a plan and you're confused, you want to take action but that feeling of "I don't know how" makes you feel anxious and nervous.

How And Where To Start?

Any self-made successful person took action... the right action for them... the right action for their own unique situation. There's no one size fits all plan!

But there's a sure path that anyone can (and shall) go through to put up a rock-solid plan to turn around their lives.

This path boils down to having clear answers to those four key questions:

1. Where am I now?

2. Why am I there?

3. Where do I want to be?

4. How to get there?

You just need to reflect on those questions and answer them clearly and honestly. To guide you on this journey, I am offering you a free digital copy of my best-seller on personal finance and investing – The 4 Stages of Building Wealth – which could be downloaded from www.employeemil lionaire.com/the4stages.

For those who would like to read this book on their kindle, you can still purchase your copy from Amazon by following this link: www.amazon.co m/Stages-Building-Wealth-Achieve-Financial-ebook/dp/B07KZLRZVK.

Trust me, who you'll become in the process is as important as the results you want to achieve in your life.

I know what you're feeling and thinking right now because I've been there:

- You might think that your current job is a limitation or an obstacle to your success. I tell you that it can be your biggest leverage if you know how to make your job work smart for you.

- You might be afraid of failure because you don't have the right support and guidance. I tell you that support and guidance will be available to you when you're ready and have the right mindset to start taking action.

- You might think you lack the right knowledge and expertise to put up an action plan and then work on it. I tell you that knowledge is readily available by reading books, attending online courses, joining webinars, or even working with a coach.

- You might feel you don't have time to take action. Trust me... all you need is a strong enough "big why" and time will find you.

I invite you to look again at your "Big Why" and go through any of the limiting beliefs that you're still struggling to overcome. If you need any help from me, I am happy to jump on a short discovery call and discuss your limiting beliefs and we can both decide if it makes sense for both of us to work together toward coaching you to overcome those obstacles that you've created to yourself and then draft a rat race exit plan. Here is the link to schedule a call with me: www.employeemillionaire.com/book-call.

I know what it means to be depressed, anxious, frustrated, and broke. But, it doesn't have to remain like that!

We all have a family who depends on us and we want to try our best to provide the best they deserve, and not to be seen as a failure by the people we love the most.

I was broke till my mid 30's, and then by following simple, yet powerful, strategies, I was able to become financially independent in a few years. If I could do it, anyone can!

Chapter Seventeen
Bridging The Gap For An Independent Retirement

When we envision what our retirement will be like, we tend to imagine that pivot point when we will no longer be working, and have the freedom to plan our days, weeks, and months to our own desires. Most of us fall short of realizing that our retirement could last 30 years or more. This means we need to plan ahead for being financially comfortable for our entire retirement.

Before we retire, while we're still making money and building our assets, we need to think through the long-term issues that will give us the most security possible for decades, not just the first few years. The highest risk issue is inflation.

Inflation Eroding our Savings

The cost of living (the price of food, clothing, oil, insurance, and rent) will keep on rising over time. If inflation averages 3% a year, what costs you $3,000 a month today will cost you more than double 5 years down the line.

The question we need to ask ourselves: Do we have the income (or enough savings) to cover the increasing cost of living over our retirement years?

High inflation isn't going away. According to a report published by Forbes in February 2022, prices are going up at their fastest rate since the early 1980s. According to the most recent Consumer Price Index (CPI) report in 2021, we are experiencing the highest inflation since February 1982.

The Golden Nest is Not Enough!

Most people think about saving money to support their retirement age, but very few think of owning income-producing assets that will keep on paying them income as long as they hold onto them.

When it comes to saving for retirement, almost everyone has a kind of saving plan, but also many fall short of this plan. According to a 2021 report from JP Morgan, only 35% of savers follow through on their saving plan and keep up with it. The main reason people can't save as much as they should is that they're spending much more than they're earning. This is mostly due to a combination of not earning enough and high spending patterns on debt and discretionary expenses.

If you are serious about wanting to save more for retirement, you need to be more conscious about your spending. You may find you can cut out certain discretionary spending. Trimming spending across multiple items will add up.

While playing the game defensively and saving for retirement is a good thing to do, taking a bit of an offensive approach by increasing our streams of residual income is always a wiser and more secure approach.

When it comes to your earned income from a job, you're not in full control of pay raises. At best you can seek another better-paying job. On the other hand, you're in full control of creating multiple streams of residual income, which are generated from income-producing assets.

Building Up Your Assets Column is Not a Luxury Anymore!

One of the main distinctions between the wealthy and the middle class is that the former own income-producing assets that will feed them for life. On the other hand, the poor and the middle class tend to have liabilities that will continue to eat their savings and income for years to come.

This should be a wake-up call to start owning income-producing assets that will keep on paying us residual income and increase our net worth.

What's Next?

If you are ready to seriously consider those retirement realities today, I think it will help you make smart decisions that will make your retirement more secure. Making a move today that reduces your living costs and increases your streams of income will reduce not just your stress, but will also reduce the worry of your adult kids.

Chapter Eighteen
What Life-Changing Advice I Would Give My 21-Year-Old Self

21 IS THE AGE at which every one of us is starting. We're full of ambitions and potential. We don't have many scars that might hold us back. This is a very personal question. Everyone has different life experiences, backgrounds, shortcomings, and ambitions. My advice to myself probably will be a lot different than yours, but I'm sure it will trigger your thought process about what you'd tell yourself—what could you have done better or differently?

At 21, I was doing my Master's Degree and at the same time working the night shift to be able to pay for my expensive tuition. I started doing the 9 to 5 grind before graduation and learned that a paycheck would never last till the end of the following month. I had no savings, but also I didn't have any debt. At that time, I did pretty well overall, but if I had a time machine, here is some advice for my younger self.

1. Networking

As a natural introvert, networking was one of my areas for self-improvement. Building relationships with new people is not my comfort zone, but I naturally tend to form lasting friendships with those I already know. I would tell my younger self to put more effort into networking, working within a team, and learning from more experienced older people (or mentors).

I was always much more comfortable talking to my peer group than to those with much higher positions and work experience. I think having mentors and role models early in my career would have accelerated my career growth in the long run.

When I was in my mid-30s and learned the importance of networking, working with teams, and seeking the guidance of mentors and coaches, my life transformed. I was able to leverage other people's experience, knowledge, time, and connections to 10X my results. Of course, each of the people whom I worked with also benefited from our business relationship. It was always a win-win arrangement.

2. Learn How to Delay Gratification

We all kind of followed a script handed over to us by our parents. We tend to value, first and foremost, a good job with a steady paycheck, good health, and retirement perks. When our income increases, we start seeking comfort and want things that give us instant gratification. Who doesn't like to wear designer brands, drive luxurious cars, live in a renowned neighbor-hood, travel on vacations, and enjoy their hobbies?

Many times, it's easy to give in to our desire for comfort. But if I could talk to my younger self, I would give myself the advice of sacrificing short-term gratification and prioritizing my goals. Most of us dream of having a great life and retiring wealthy, but we keep it as a dream or wish and never put it at the top of our goals. That's because we all find refuge in the easier objectives of security and comfort instead of bothering with the effort and **education** required to become successful.

Both security and comfort are short-term thinking for the poor and middle class, where a paycheck, health insurance, retirement plan, a house, a car, entertainment, and travel all offer instant gratification. On the other hand, the wealthy have developed the discipline of sacrificing short-term indulgence and investing their time into their financial literacy. As a consequence, they enjoy much better and bigger things in the future. Their delayed gratification is way more rewarding.

3. Become Financially Literate

When I first joined the corporate world, it was challenging to work at night and study during the day, but at the same time a lot of fun. I was like a dry sponge, learning everything about running a business from the ground up. I met many interesting and smart people—and each taught me something about business. Still, none could teach me something about personal finance, just because most people are not in control of their personal finances.

The income was nice, too, but I could never save and never knew where my income was being spent. I knew I was always waiting for the next paycheck to get out of financial stress, pay my bills, or make the minimum installment towards a loan or my credit card statement!

Earning good money before graduating was a nice start, but I think it was a mistake never to receive any financial education to control my cash flow. Now that I know more, I would tell my younger self to become financially literate before earning my first-ever paycheck to become a real pilot who's in control of his finances. We develop bad money habits from the point we start earning an income and never know how to invest it to build our net worth.

4. Self Discipline

Most of us become disciplined in our work because someone else is watching us. We learn this at school, home, and even work. This is not self-discipline!

When self-disciplined, you do what you must, even if you've only made your promise to yourself. Consistency is harder when no one is clapping for you. It would be best if you clapped for yourself during those times. Be your biggest fan!

I will advise my younger self never to wait to get in the mood to start working on a new project or task. Here's the truth: you are never going to be in the mood 100% unless you decide that you will do something. Act on what you need to do. Don't give yourself enough time to reason or talk yourself out of what you ought to do.

5. Create a Baby Steps Routine Towards Your Long Term Goals

I don't know why, as young adults, we tend to think we can shoot for the moon, and even if we miss, we will reach the stars! With this thinking, we tend to set unachievable deadlines or goals, leading to failure. For some reason, we keep this mentality and repeat setting unrealistic goals until we fail too many times, and then we get demotivated and lose our confidence.

I will give my younger self life-transforming advice to think of his "Big Why"... this laser-focused strong thing that will make me move towards something I want in life. When this becomes clear, my younger self will realize that money is only an enabler to achieve greater things. I learned that my personal ambitions came first, before my financial ambitions. I discovered that my financial ambitions acted as enablers for me to achieve my personal ambitions.

Look ahead to 3 to 5 years from now—even dare to envision yourself 10 years from now. Think about how your life will look. Are your actions today directing you toward your "Big Why?"

I will advise my younger self to set realistic yet challenging long-term goals. I will whisper a secret to my younger self to break every task into baby steps, so I don't procrastinate. Consistent actions toward our goals will transform into a habit or a routine to plan our work and work our plan. It's much better to do one small step at a time than to try to do a lot and get stuck in the end.

6. Create Accountability

Be more accountable to your goals by letting other people know about them. Share your goals, ambitions, and even plans with someone you trust. This could be a colleague, friend, partner, mentor, or coach.

The simple act of sharing your goals and then trying to save face by making things happen—even if those actions appear overwhelming—will help you create self-accountability.

If this other mentor is more experienced, a mentor, or a coach who dares you do something beyond your comfort zone that will take you closer to your goals, you've got a healthy way of making things happen.

Chapter Nineteen

How To 10X Your Results With The Help Of A Mentor

NEED ADVICE AND MENTORSHIP for your next career step, investment, or entrepreneurial start-up? Make sure you follow the steps of someone who's been there and done that.

We're living in one of the most blessed times in human history. We can study anything we want, where we want, and whenever we want, with a few clicks on our screens or voice commands on our devices. To put things into perspective, that was quite impossible a few decades ago, even for the most influential people, the royalties, and the people with the highest education level.

This big opportunity also comes with the challenges of many "claimed experts" pitching their services for a fee. There is so much information out there, and everyone is getting extremely confused and overwhelmed. It's becoming harder to realize what's real and what's not. That's a problem, leading you to block everything around you and eventually miss the opportunity to have the right mentor guiding you.

Unfortunately, so many scammers are out there, with clever marketing campaigns bombarding you on social media and even on Google! It's becoming almost impossible to avoid them popping up on your screen. Many of those impostors are getting rich by making you feel good and motivated, but with no actionable lessons.

How to find a mentor that's right for you?

Ready to get started? Here are the top tips for finding a mentor to help you 10x your potential.

1. Go for the "been there, done that" type of mentor

When choosing a mentor, it pays to go with the "been there, done that" type. Go for someone who has had a good share of mistakes and failures but has eventually emerged as a winner.

A mentor's role is to share valuable lessons from previous experiences—the good, the bad, and the ugly—and attempt to instill a drive from which you can learn to improve your career, life, or business. This will speed up your personal growth.

A mentor should truly care for their students by making them stand in front of a mirror and understand their strengths and weaknesses. Mentors would help their students leverage their strengths, acknowledge their weaknesses, and overcome them.

Mentors should have a track record similar to what they want to achieve. Their background (before their success), failures, and successes should inspire and impress you.

This makes you admire and respect them, thus pushing you to follow their guidance.

2. Choose a mentor who challenges you

Good mentors should challenge their mentees to get out of their comfort zone. You won't learn anything new and exciting if your mentor can't make you see things from new and different perspectives.

Before making your final pick, make sure the one you've chosen shares similar experience threads with you - whether there are challenges they managed to overcome or mistakes they've learned from in the past.

Mentors provide technical and experimental support and should also help you ask the right questions, which will help you get the right answers.

A mentor's job is to help you overcome challenges in a completely new and unique way—a way that they've used for themselves or their students and that has worked well for them.

This means they have a bulletproof strategy and process you can trust and follow without being exposed to unnecessary risks—without losing time and money on trial and error.

The more their process or system is documented or published, and the more it is acknowledged by third-party critiques and testimonials from other students, the more legit it is.

3. Find that special someone you admire and relate to

Generally, a mentor should consider you a colleague who will listen and help you achieve your career goals.

It should be someone:

- you can talk openly about your ideas without any red tape,

- who will celebrate your successes and

- who will mitigate your fears.

Mentors should help you in achieving skills away from the bench. They will push you to go out and network with others from your industry so that you will find the help and support you might need before you need it.

All good mentors are also willing to be mentored themselves and understand that there is always room for improvement in training others. This is a two-way highway where a mentor helps and guides others. With an open mind, they would perfect their style, hold your hands, and walk you through all the steps and hiccups you might encounter until you achieve the goals that you have set.

4. Find a mentor who puts themselves in your shoes

There are many cases where great mentors have done a poor job for their students despite having the knowledge, experience, and process required to make them fit as great mentors. The missing ingredients were the art of teaching, patience, and listening, which all boils down to the fact that they could not relate to their students despite the fact they were in the same hole at one point.

This is one of the most important, yet often ignored, aspects when people are looking for mentors. They then end up disappointed and confused because they realize they can't relate to their mentor's teaching and coaching style.

So, make sure that you consider this as well when you get someone to become your mentor. Look at their content, observe their teaching style, check their behavior, and see if they have patience and time when explaining the same thing repeatedly—each time from a slightly different angle—until they make sure you grasp a certain concept.

5. Pick a mentor who is interested in your advancement

One of the first signs that show whether a mentor is a good fit for you and whether they care about you can be observed when you first meet them face to face, through a phone call, or on a video call.

Pay attention and see if they will ask you the right questions and if they want to learn more about you—your current situation, your ambitions, your motivations, and why you want to achieve what you want.

The next step, which would give you a clear STOP or GO signal, will be to find out if they have ever refused anybody. If they refuse people, that means they are true and honest with their work and their students. If they claim and think they can teach everyone all the time, I tell you that's impossible, and that is a sign for you to run away from them immediately!

6. An informal (yet structured) relationship works best with a mentor

People respond better, feel better, look better, and understand better when they can be themselves without being obliged to act in ways different from their natural behaviors.

It's better to have a mentor with whom you can be open and discuss everything you have in your mind. A good connection with your mentor will improve everything, and results will come faster than you can expect!

Similarly, a great mentor will make you feel relaxed, open, and close to them due to their positive attitude and their lack of fear of sharing their failures.

This kind of close relationship allows mentors to openly guide their students, push them to find their answers at times, keep them on track, and highlight the negative stuff that goes in their heads and behaviors.

7. Make sure you are a coachable person

It doesn't matter what mentor you choose. You can have the best in the world, but it will be useless unless you're coachable.

I want to tackle this topic since few seem to talk about it. There are some situations when you are the problem and not the mentor! Being coachable is one of life's most important skills and attitudes, whether or not you're an athlete.

If you wish to grow, learn, improve, excel, or peak perform, you should care about whether or not you're coachable. In other words, being coachable relates to a happy, productive life.

It means you're ready to change, transform, improve, or excel—whatever that means for you and your situation.

Being coachable means you're open to listening to feedback, receiving constructive criticism without taking it personally, willing to look at your performance to improve it, and generally, a super-badass-enthusiastic go-getter type of person.

You must respectfully listen to your mentor and avoid the tricky mindset of "I already know this."

To make sure you get the most out of your coaching and take the right amount of action, I have some important advice:

Avoid The Syndrome of "I Already Know This."

I used to think, "I already know this"!

Whenever you feel you are lying to yourself with thoughts such as "I Already Know This," ask yourself those three questions:

#1: Am I Doing It?

#2: Have I Mastered It?

#3: Do My Results Prove I Am Doing It & Have Mastered It?

If you answered "No" to any of the above questions, then you haven't mastered this topic yet, and your results prove that.

Regardless of where we fall on the success ladder, we all still need guidance, mentorship, and coaching. CEOs of the largest corporations have mentors and coaches—they need them.

Big egos get the hardest punches from life because there's no other way to learn or realize how toxic this is for them and the people around them. Being coachable while leaving your ego at the door is about awareness and the ability to take the golden nuggets from a situation and use them to your advantage.

Being coachable is wisdom. It means paying attention to other people and their experience, wisdom, skills, and knowledge.

It pays to listen and learn from others, regardless of how developed your skills are. Be willing to listen closely enough to see what might help you on your journey.

The mentor-mentee relationship is all about give and take. Ensure you listen and, more importantly, put their advice into action. A good mentor will hold you accountable and push you to succeed, so don't waste their time. This will be key to a good long-term mentoring relationship that works for both of you.

Now that you know how to find a mentor, start looking for the right one.

Having a skilled mentor can get you closer to your goals.

Final Note - Take Action and Change Your Life

Across all the limiting beliefs discussed in this book, the underlying personal truths were fear, cynicism, laziness, arrogance, ignorance, or bad habits.

I encourage you to keep on doing those self-talks and uncovering those personal truths to avoid letting them become obstacles between you and your empowering beliefs.

Please write down your personal beliefs, unravel your personal truths, and consider their respective empowering beliefs.

I will leave you now with a question, which I trust you will reflect on and hopefully make meaningful changes to your finances and life.

Will You Take Action and Change Your Life?

Once you figure out the answer to this question, don't get caught in "the captivity of passivity," get out there and make it happen.

Take action!

Seek the Help of Coaches and Mentors

It is amazing how a coach can help you figure out the important things in life you want to achieve and how a mentor can help you achieve those goals. While digging in my notes, I found a simple definition that differentiates a coach from a mentor – "A coach has some great questions for your answers; a mentor has some great answers for your questions." The coaches I worked with throughout my life asked me many challenging questions that triggered my thoughts and made me look for answers. In parallel, I have worked with great mentors who have helped me with the answers to the questions triggered by my coaches.

I hope this book has achieved its objectives of enabling me to be both your coach and your mentor at other times. My objective in this book is to share my learning and experience, which have enabled me to achieve financial freedom. Without the help of coaches and mentors, my mistakes could have been numerous, and I might not have achieved whatever success I have achieved so far.

Thank you for taking the time to read this book. I hope you will apply the concepts shared in it to your investment career. You can always visit www.employeemillionaire.com/breakout-resources to access the different forms and templates that have been shared in this book.

Please also feel free to reach out if you need any assistance, coaching, or mentoring in your personal finances and rental property investment journey. My team and I are excited to work alongside you and witness your success in the future. Simply visit us at www.employeemillionaire.com/book-call to book a complimentary strategy and discovery call with us.

Review Request

THANK YOU SO MUCH for reading this book. I realize millions of books are out there, and I want to express my infinite appreciation for your choosing mine.

Now that you have finished reading this book, it would be a huge favor to me and future readers if you left feedback on Amazon.

If you enjoyed this book (and I think you did if you got to the end), please leave a review—this is one of the only ways authors like myself can find readers like you.

If you wish to write a review (and I hope you do), you can do that in any of the following three ways:

- Visit the Amazon review page of this book: www.amazon.com/gp/product-review/B08S2ZXR3P

- Select this book from my Amazon author page: www.amazon.com/author/hjchammas

- Go to this page on my domain, and you will be redirected to the Amazon review page of this book: www.employeemillionaire.com/review-mmsh

About H.J. Chammas

H. J. Chammas is an award-winning best-selling author and self-made "Employee Millionaire" who has achieved financial freedom by investing in rental properties throughout Asia, Dubai, and Europe. With over 14 years of industry and investing experience, he brings forward a blueprint for investing in rental properties in a simple and clear manner.

H. J. Chammas lives with his wife Joyce and their son, Ryan, in Dubai. Both are active real estate investors specializing in rental properties.

You can find more about H. J. Chammas at

www.employeemillionaire.com

More from H.J. Chammas

If you have enjoyed this book, we hope you'll take a moment to check out some of the other great material offered by *The Employee Millionaire*. This is my way of leveraging my time to be able to help as many people as possible. Some of those materials are video courses you can study at your own pace and the crème de la crème solution is working with me on a one-on-one coaching journey to help you get out of your current financial challenges towards becoming financially independent and the next *employee millionaire*.

4 Pillars of Wealth Course

The 4 Pillars of Wealth course is your 4-month financial success guide to paying off bad debt, repairing your credit, creating residual income, and growing your wealth to achieve financial independence.

This course is for you if:

- You're doing the 9 to 5 grind because you have to.

- You're stuck with a salary that your boss decides whether it gets increased.

- You're struggling to make ends meet, with no money left from your income to pay your bills, debt, and expenses.

- You're trading long hours of your day, most days of the year, working for a job that has stripped you down from the time to live your life.

With *The 4 Pillars of Wealth* course you'll be able to:

- ***Repair your credit and attract capital*** - Improve your credit score and financing eligibility to attract the necessary capital to fund your investments. You'll learn the hacks on how to fund your investments with bad credit so you can quickly get that down payment and start creating residual income and become financially independent.

- ***Develop a winning mindset*** - Overcome the limiting beliefs that are making you stand in your own way to Financial Success. Discover how to quickly avoid the #1 mistake investors make that causes them to take months or years to get started, so you can complete your first investment in just a few weeks.

- ***Select cash-flowing investments*** - Determine the investment vehicles that are the best fit for your objectives and that will pay you new streams of income and grow your wealth.

- ***Increase your passive income to a level you can quit your job*** - Discover my proven process that will increase your total income and save you from the piles of debt and bills so that you stop trading too many hours for few dollars and free up more of your time to see more of your family and travel the world.

Everything is online and you can learn at your own pace.

Check it out on www.employeemillionaire.com/fourpillarscourse

The Employee Millionaire Real Estate Investor Course

The Employee Millionaire course is your step-by-step guide to owning at least 3 cash-flowing rental properties in one Year.

This course is for you if:

- You're dealing with bad credit and high Debt to Income ratio.

- You're trapped in the rat race since you started your career.

- You want to have the freedom to enjoy life on your terms.

This course is a simple rental property investing guide, even if you're starting with bad credit, no down payment, and zero knowledge.

With *The Employee Millionaire* course you'll be able to:

- ***Repair your credit and find capital to invest with other peoples' money*** - Restructure your monthly debt payments, pay off all your debt, repair your bad credit, and improve your creditworthiness to attract the necessary capital to fund your investments.

- ***Develop a millionaire mindset and success habits*** - Overcome limiting beliefs that have been stopping you from the Financial Success you deserve.

- ***Increase your passive income to a level you can quit your job, if you choose to*** - Finance, own, rent, and manage at least 3 rental properties (that will pay you monthly passive income) in your first year.

- ***Scale up your cash-flowing property portfolio with a solid system*** - Work from your home and spend more time with your family. Increase your net worth to a million dollars in less than 3 years!

    Check it out on www.employeemillionaire.com/VCP

The Employee Millionaire Inner Circle

Join my Inner Circle where you will have personal access to me to answer all your questions and guide you on your rental property investments. With this level of guidance, you will minimize all time and money that could be lost by trial and error.

The Employee Millionaire Inner Circle is for individuals who are serious about achieving their financial independence with a personalized approach.

- Learn powerful, time-tested concepts surrounding wealth creation through investing in rental properties.

- Work with a coach who will guide you and make you accountable for applying the concepts to your own unique situation.

- Work with a coach who is committed to your success and is eager to assist you in any way we can.

- Move from mere theory to application, thus establishing new behavior patterns that are embraced by all professional real estate investors.

- Change your financial situation and become a confident rental property investor.

There are very limited openings for the Inner Circle. Apply now by scheduling a discovery session with me. We will discuss your possible options on this call.

www.employeemillionaire.com/book-call